Kindle Paperwhite User Guide 2023

The Perfect Kindle Paperwhite Manual for
Beginners, Seniors, and New Kindle Users

Ian Allan

First published in 2023 by Geocode Mapping and Analysis Pty Ltd, Melbourne. Australia

Copyright Geocode Mapping and Analysis Pty Ltd, 2023

The moral rights of the author have been asserted.

National Library of Australia Cataloguing-in-Publication data: Creator: Allan. Ian. 1963 – author.

Title: Kindle Paperwhite User Guide 2023

Subtitle: The Perfect Kindle Paperwhite Manual for Beginners, Seniors, and New Kindle Users

ISBN:

Notes: Includes table of contents.

Subjects: kindle paperwhite

Disclaimer

The material in this publication is general in nature only. It does not represent professional advice. Everybody's circumstances are different. If expert assistance is required, the service of an appropriate professional should be sought. To the maximum extent permitted by law, the author and publisher disclaim all responsibility and liability to any person, arising directly or indirectly from them taking or not taking action based on the information in this publication.

Ian Allan is not affiliated with and does not endorse any of the corporate entities mentioned in or involved in the distribution of this work, or any third party entities whose trademarks and logos may appear on this work.

The menus and techniques I've written about were correct at the time of my last edit (July 2023). However, Amazon often updates its menus, apps and website. So, some items might have changed, and the Amazon website might be different between where you live and where I live.

About the author

I got the knack for teaching technolo-gy when I was one of a small team of software engineers on 24 hour technical support for a major Australian bank in the 1980s. Later I became a favorite of my geography students at a tier 1 Aus-tralian university. None of these Arts fac-ulty students had any technical experi-  ence, but I got them all to understand the basics of computer mapping . . . and enthused a number to pursue my one-semester minor as their career. These days, I have 9000 or so geography students on the Udemy teaching platform.

Too many teachers suffer from the curse-of-knowledge. That's where they assume that if something is simple for them, then it must also be simple for everybody else. That's not me. I'm good at breaking down the overwhelming into smaller manageable parts. I hope you come to agree as you read through my Kindle Paper-white User Guide 2023.

Ian
August 2023

Contents

Chapter 1

Introduction

I love my Kindle Paperwhite.

I love that it's waterproof - I can read by the water and in the bath. I love that its touch screen - the tiny buttons on my old kindle were driving me crazy.

I love that it's backlit – no more book light.

I love that it's e-ink – it's so easy on my eyes, and I can easily adjust the screen brightness and font size.

I love that I can highlight text and take notes while I'm reading – that's great for nonfiction.

I love that I can search for any word or term – in a book, in my library, or even in the kindle store.

I love that I can move seamlessly between Kindle apps and Kindle devices – Amazon's Whispersync cloud sees to that.

I love that my books are safe – if I lose my paperwhite, my books, notes and highlights are all stored in the cloud.

I love the massive bookstore that sits behind my paperwhite – most books are reasonably priced and some are even free. I read more widely and more often than I ever did.

I love that my paperwhite is lightweight and slim - it easily slips into the front pocket of my bag.

Finally, *I love* that my paperwhite is a reading tool that knows its place - it does what its meant to do, and it does it well.

Yes, there's a lot to love about my paperwhite. Did I mention that *I love* my paperwhite?

Enough of the prose. They're all the things that I'm going to talk about in this book.

In the remainder of chapter 1, I give you an overview of how you can get the most out of your paperwhite, and which chapters are most likely to be relevant to you.

In Chapter 2, I give you a first-use overview.

In Chapter 3, I take you through the setup procedure step-by-step.

In Chapter 4, I take you on a tour of your paperwhite - the different screens and toolbars, and how to read your first book.

In Chapter 5, I talk about your paperwhite as a learning aid – dictionary, Wikipedia, and translation functionality, as well as X-Ray, text highlighting and note taking.

In Chapter 6, I talk about adjusting the appearance of your screen – fonts, text size, screen orientation, and more.

In Chapter 7, I'll show you how to bring both Amazon and non-Amazon content onto your paperwhite. How to use the Kindle store, and how to send books to your Paperwhite using e-mail, the cloud and USB cable.

Chapter 8 is devoted to the Settings menu - dictionaries, languages, accessibility, parental controls, and more.

In Chapter 9, I talk about managing your Paperwhite from a browser and take you on a tour of the free browser reader. The browser reader is a great place to review your notes and highlights, and see color versions of all your book covers.

In Chapter 10, I talk about types of subscriptions and categories of books in the Amazon store. Understanding these can help you squeeze the most out of your paperwhite experience. In Chapter 11, I deal with a bunch of troubleshooting problems.

Finally, in Chapter 12, I answer a bunch of Frequently Asked Questions.

There's also nine figures that you can download from ianall anauthor.com/paperwhite. I refer to the figures a lot in the text. To make it a bit easier for you, each label is unique.

OK, let's get cracking.

1.1 – Use Amazon's ecosystem to get the most out of your paperwhite

Much like some people use a car for Sunday drives and other people are always searching for a car's turbo-boost button, your paperwhite can be used for pleasure-reads or, by harnessing Amazon's ecosystem, it can become a powerful and flexible reading tool. In a nutshell, those two extremes are what this book is about.

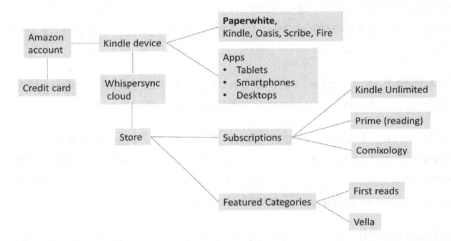

Figure 1-1: A diagram showing Amazon's ecosystem.
Amazon's ecosystem relies on you being logged into your account so it can curate content for you, and synchronize all your books across all your Kindle devices. You can download this figure from ianallanauthor.com/paperwhite.

At this point, it's worth taking the time for a 30,000-foot overview of amazon's ecosystem as it applies to eBooks. By ecosystem, I mean, enabled by the cloud, everything that's linked to your Amazon account - subscriptions, content and device management from your web browser, and synchronized purchasing, reading, highlighting and note taking functionality across your paperwhite and other Kindle apps and devices. Let's look at the ecosystem components...

- **Ecosystem component 1 - Subscriptions:** If you read two or more books a month, I strongly encourage you to consider becoming a Prime member or a Kindle Unlimited subscriber (Chapter 10). Prime members have thousands of books to choose from. Kindle Unlimited subscribers have millions of books to choose from. Some books even come bundled with narration.

- **Ecosystem component 2 - Book recommendations:** Amazon uses your reading history to curate lists of book recommendations. The Kindle app, Amazon store in a web browser, and paperwhite have different ways of showing them. If you like to read widely, be sure to alternate between the kindle stores on your paperwhite, the apps (eg. on your smartphone or desktop), and the amazon store in a web browser (logged out of amazon and in private mode too).

- **Ecosystem component 3 - Content and device management from a browser:** You can manage your books and what's on your paperwhite and every kindle device from your web browser. You can also view your purchasing and borrowing histories (Chapter 9).

- **Ecosystem component 4 - Synchronized reading across all your kindle apps, your paperwhite and other kindle devices:** There's a Kindle app for most smart phones, tablets, and desktops. You can also read Kindle books in a web browser. Thanks to Whispersync, your purchases, reading, note taking and highlighting are synchronized across all your apps and devices in near-real time.

- **Ecosystem component 5 - Overcoming your paper-**

white's limitations: Paperwhites are great e-readers, but beyond that, they can be clunky. However, amazon's ecosystem allows you to use kindle apps and the amazon website to overcome these limitations. Here's three limitations. . .

◦ **Audio:** Some Kindle books come bundled with audio - the Kindle apps are much better suited to audiobook listening (Chapter 8).
◦ **Note taking:** I do basic highlighting and note taking on my paperwhite (Chapter 5). I edit these in the Kindle apps (Chapter 6).
◦ **Account management:** You can only do basic account management on your paperwhite - a web browser is much better suited to this (Chapter 9).

1.2 - How to get the most out of this book

You may find it useful to have your Paperwhite in front of you while you read or listen to this book. Some of the topics may seem a little abstract otherwise. Whenever possible, I list the path to a menu in italics directly under each section heading. In the audiobook, I explain each path.

Chapter 11 has extensive troubleshooting help. And, I talk you through the menus. Not only describing them, but also explaining how you might use them, and why they're important. Also, for the few things that your paperwhite is not good at, I suggest alternatives because I want to help you to avoid being frustrated and wasting your time.

While reading this book, you could use the search bar (label (29) in Figure 4-4) to find topics that interest you. However, I refer to

Figure 4-1 thru Figure 6-1 a lot. I suggest that you bookmark each of them (label (28) in Figure 4-4) so you can return to them easily. You can also download a printable pdf of the figures from .

Here's some ideas for how different readers might make the most use of this book...

- **If you just want to get started, look at...**

  ◦ The 5-minute QuickStart in Chapter 2.
  ◦ Setting up your paperwhite in Chapter 3.
  ◦ Buying and reading your first Kindle book in Chapter 4.
  ◦ Troubleshooting screen taps in Chapter 11.

- **If you're a language learner, look at. . .**

  ◦ Inbuilt dictionary, X-Ray and vocabulary builder in Chapter 5.
  ◦ Continuous word definitions and Word Wise in Chapter 6.
  ◦ Setting up languages, translations and dictionaries in Chapter 8.

- **If you're a nonfiction reader, look at. . .**

  ◦ Note taking and highlighting on your paperwhite in Chapter 5.
  ◦ Note taking and highlighting in the kindle cloud reader in Chapter 9.
  ◦ Organizing your books into collections in Chapter 7.

- **If you need the accessibility features, look at. . .**

  ◦ Font size and dyslexic font in Chapter 6.
  ◦ Voice view screen and menu reader in Chapter 8.

- **Ideally, everybody should understand Amazon's ecosystem. Look at. . .**

  ◦ Note taking in Chapter 5.
  ◦ Buying books on your smartphone and transferring books from your computer in Chapter 7.
  ◦ Managing your paperwhite from a web browser in Chapter 9.
  ◦ Amazon subscriptions explained in Chapter 10.

Chapter 2

Five minute setup and overview

Here's a birds-eye view of setting up your Paperwhite. This chapter is for someone who is used to installing software and setting up and using new devices. For the less experienced, Chapter 3 goes into greater detail. For many people, their paperwhite setup will be trouble free and intuitive. It can take less than 5 minutes! Let's get you up and running. Here goes. . .

Charging: You charge your paperwhite from the port in its base using the cable that came with it. It will charge from most USB chargers. For me, that's my iPhone charger, computer port and the USB port in my car. An amber light near the charging port means that it's charging, and a green light means that it's fully charged.

Powering up: The power button is around an inch to the right of the charging port. Depress it until you see a green light and your paperwhite will power up.

Setup: If you bought your Paperwhite directly from Amazon and ticked the *link to your account* box when you checked out, then you will only need to connect to your Wi-Fi from the Wi-Fi list that pops up during setup. However, if you bought your paperwhite from your local retailer, you will be stepped through a setup process that also includes signing up to the goodreads book review site and signing into your Amazon account.

First use: When setup is complete, you will be taken to the *Home* screen. Notice the three items at the bottom. *Home* on the left, a book thumbnail in the middle, and *Library* on the right.

- **Home:** Tap *Home* on the left side of the bottom menu bar to be taken to the *Home* screen. The *Home* screen includes zones such as *From your library* – they're the most recent books that you've accessed. There's also a bunch of other categories that Amazon curates for you based on what it knows about your reading preferences.

  If you tap on a book in the *Home* screen, the book will open if you own it. Otherwise, you will be taken to the book's sales page where you can view more information about it or buy it.

- **Book thumbnail:** In the middle of the bottom menu bar is a thumbnail of the most recent book that you have been reading. Tap on this to open the book.

- **Library:** Tap *Library* on the right side of the bottom menu bar to be taken to the *Library* screen. It has thumbnails of all the books you own, or have borrowed from Prime Reading or Kindle Unlimited. If you are new to Kindle, this might only contain a couple of free books, compliments of Amazon. If you tap on a book in here, the book will open.

In an open book. . .

- Pinch two fingers together or drag them apart to change the text size.

- Tap the right side of the screen to go to the next page.

- Tap the left side of the screen to go to the previous page.

- Swipe down from the top of the screen to see the screen warmth slider (gen 11 only), and screen brightness slider.

- Tap the top of the screen to reveal the *Standard* toolbar. There's a back-arrow in its top left corner that you can tap to exit the book, and be taken back to either the *Home screen* or *Library screen*.

Some icons are contextual: By that I mean that they link to menus that are relevant to the task you are doing at the time. For example, the three vertical dots icon (:) launches different menus from your *Home* screen and *Library* screen, from within a book, and from the menu that pops up when you highlight text within a passage.

Context also comes into play when you tap, hold and release on a word, phrase, or passage. If you've selected a noun in an X-Ray enabled book, the X-Ray menu pops up and you can find all the passages in the book where the noun is mentioned. Selecting any other word launches the in-built dictionary, as well as options to see it's Wikipedia entry or the translation menu. Or, you could just highlight a passage and use the keyboard that appears to write notes about it.

Weaknesses: For all the things I love about my paperwhite, it does have its weaknesses. Fortunately, these tend to be strengths in the Kindle apps. For example, taking notes is a little clunky on your paperwhite, but they're easy to revise (and even color-code) in any one of the kindle apps.

Your amazon account: In a browser, be sure to familiarize your-self with the *Content and Devices* area of your amazon account. That's where you can look at your purchasing, and Prime and Kindle Unlimited borrowing history, and set up email permissions for transferring non-amazon content to your paperwhite.

Well, that should be enough to get you up-and-running. Like many things in life, though, the devil is in the detail. I began this book by laying out all the reasons why I love my Paperwhite. In the rest of this book I'll unpack all the functionality that I mentioned there. There's labelled screen captures to make it easy for you to see what I'm talking about. You can also download a printable PDF of these from .

Read on and we'll get into the nuts and bolts.

Chapter 3

Detailed setup

This chapter is an in-depth treatment of how to setup your paperwhite. If your paperwhite connected successfully to Wi-Fi and your Amazon account, and you can open a book, then you should skip to the next chapter. Otherwise, read on to be shown what to expect when you power up your paperwhite for the first time. There are three setup scenarios. . ..

- **Setup scenario 1 - Your paperwhite was setup by amazon at checkout:** If you bought your paperwhite directly from Amazon and clicked on the *Link to my account* box at checkout, you will only need to charge it, power it up, and connect it to Wi-Fi.

- **Setup scenario 2 - First use auto setup:** If you bought your paperwhite from somewhere other than Amazon, you will be guided through a 7 step setup process.

- **Setup scenario 3 - Manual setup**: You go down this path if the auto-setup did not work for you.

The days of needing a technical person to set up a device for you are mostly gone. Setting up a paperwhite is a trouble-free exercise for most people. But there can be problems. Chapter 11 includes a bunch of troubleshooting tips.

3.1 - Before your first use

There are three things that you should do before you set up your paperwhite.

- **Charging:** Make sure your paperwhite is fully charged so that it does not unexpectantly power down during setup and potentially corrupt the process.

- **Wi-Fi:** Make sure you are in range of Wi-Fi and that you have your Wi-Fi password handy.

- **Amazon account:** Have your Amazon account details handy. If you don't already have an account, in a web browser, go to your local amazon store and create one.

3.2 - Charging your paperwhite

Quickstart: Plug the cable that came bundled with your paperwhite into a power source such as a phone charger or computer. An amber light near the charging port shows that it's charging. A green light shows that it's charged.

Your Paperwhite comes with a USB cable for charging from either your computer or wall adapter. To ensure trouble-free setup, it's important to fully charge it first.

For a Gen 11 Paperwhite, a full charge takes 5 hours when connected to a computer, 2.5 hours with a 9W USB charger, or for some models, 3.5 hours with a 10W Q1 wireless charging pad. Older Paperwhites have a smaller battery and take around 2.5 hours to fully charge.

Gen 11 models use a USB-C cable and older models use a Micro-USB cable. Often the cable that comes with your Paperwhite works better than no-name cables.

An amber light near the charging point means that it's charging, and a green light means that it's fully charged.

You can use your paperwhite while its charging. A lightening bolt symbol appears in the top right corner of the screen. If you're charging from your computer, you should unmount / eject the kindle drive to avoid corrupting its memory.

See Chapter 11 to troubleshoot charging problems.

3.3 - The power button

Quickstart: To power on and power off, press the power button until you see a green light. It's an inch to the right of the charging port.

The power button at the base of your paperwhite is used to start it, place it into sleep mode, turn it off, and restart it. It can be hard to see - it's about an inch to the right of the charging port.

Starting

Press the power button and release it when you see the green light at your paperwhite's base.

Sleep mode

Place your paperwhite into sleep mode with a quick press-and-release on the power button. Press-and-release again to wake it up.

Sleep mode begins automatically after 10 minutes of inactivity. The backlight will dim, your book will close, and the screen saver will display. Whispersync remains active so some power will still be consumed.

You can also toggle sleep mode from the *settings* menu (see *Power Saver* in Chapter 8).

Shutting down

Depress the power button for 10 seconds. The green light at the base will flash. Then the amber light. From the box that appears on the screen, tap *Screen Off*. Shutting down your paperwhite turns off power consuming activity such as the backlight and Whisper-sync.

Restarting

Restarting your paperwhite is much like a reboot on your desktop computer. You may need to do this if your paperwhite freezes, or its response times become slow. It's good practice to restart any device occasionally anyhow. There's two ways to restart your Paperwhite. . .

1. Depress the power button and continue holding it in after it has powered off (allow 40 seconds).

2. Depress the power button for 10 seconds. The green light at the base will flash. Then the amber light. From the box that appears on the screen, tap *Restart.*

3.4 - First-Use Auto Setup

On its first use, your paperwhite will walk you through a setup process. To avoid setup issues, make sure its fully charged before you begin. Press the start button at its base. If you bought your Paperwhite from your Amazon account and ticked the *Link to my account* box at checkout, you will only need to connect to Wi-Fi. Otherwise, expect the following prompts. . .

1. Select a language.

2. Select a region.

3. Connect to Wi-Fi.

4. Login to your amazon account using a username and password.

   ○ If you don't already have an account, in a web browser, go to your local amazon store and create one.

5. Send a kindle app link to your smartphone.

   ○ Type in your phone number and tap *Send Link*. Amazon will send you a text with a custom link to install the kindle app. When you use this link, the app will be automagically linked to your amazon account and synced to your paperwhite.

6. Choose to create / sign in to a goodreads account using your Amazon details.

7. Choose an audible free trial if you'd like to.

8. Setup complete.

Troubleshooting your paperwhite setup:

If you accidentally chose a foreign language and you can no longer read the on-screen setup instructions, you will need to reset your paperwhite. I show you the menu path to do that in Chapter 11.

3.5 - Connecting to Wi-Fi

Home / Library > ⋮ > Settings > Wireless > Wi-Fi Networks

Quickstart: When prompted, select a Wi-Fi network and enter a password.

If you're setting up a brand new out-of-the-box paperwhite, you'll be prompted to select a Wi-Fi network to connect to and enter a password. If it connects successfully, go to the Sign into Amazon section below. Otherwise, read on.

Assuming you're in range of an active Wi-Fi network, tap the : icon (label (3) in Figure 4-1) and select *Settings* from the menu that appears, tap *Wireless, and then tap Wi-Fi Networks.* A list of available Wi-Fi networks will display, including a mobile phone hotspot if one is active. Select the network you want to connect to and enter a password when prompted. A confirmation message will display on the screen if the connection is successful.

You only need to connect to each wireless network once. Your paperwhite will automatically reconnect the next time you're in range.

3.6 - Sign into Amazon
: > *Settings* > *Your Account* > *Register Your Kindle*

Quickstart: If you bought your paperwhite directly from Amazon and clicked on the "Link to my account" box at checkout, your paperwhite is already signed into your account.

As a part of auto-setup, a *Register your kindle* box appears in the welcome screen. If it does not appear, tap the : icon (label   in Figure 4-1) and select *Settings.* Navigate to the *Your Account* menu, and then tap *Register Your Kindle* (Chapter 8).

You could use your Paperwhite without registering it on your Amazon account, but you would have to transfer all your books using a

USB cable (Chapter 7). Expect that experience to be cumbersome and frustrating. Also, the Digital Rights Management (DRM) security that is attached to most Kindle books prevents them from being read on an unregistered Kindle.

Could you spare a moment to review my book?
Don't forget the resources page at ianallanauthor.com/paperwhite

I would be so grateful if you would leave a review on Amazon. . .

Chapter 4

Paperwhite tour

So, your paperwhite is setup and ready to use. In this chapter I'll show you how to find your way around the *Home* screen, the *Book* screen and the *Library* screen, and how to buy your first book and read it.

There's labelled screen captures that I refer to often, so you might like to bookmark them (label (28) in Figure 4-4, and *4.9 - How to Bookmark a Page* towards the end of this chapter). Otherwise, use the search bar (label (29) in Figure 4-4) to find mentions of terms that interest you. You can also download the figures as a printable pdf from .

4.1 - Quickstart

Tap any book thumbnail. . .

- *In the Home screen: Get taken to the book's sales page in the Kindle store.*

- *In the Library screen: The book will open.*

When a book is open. . .

- *Tap the right side for the next page.*

- *Tap the left side for the previous page.*

- *Swipe down from the top of the screen to see the Quick Access menu. That's where you'll find the screen brightness and warmth sliders. Tap the up arrow at the bottom of the menu to exit it.*

- *Tap the top of the screen to see the Standard Toolbar. Then tap the arrow in the top left corner to return to the Home screen or Library screen.*

- *Use a pinching action to reduce and enlarge the font size.*

4.2 - The Home and Library screens

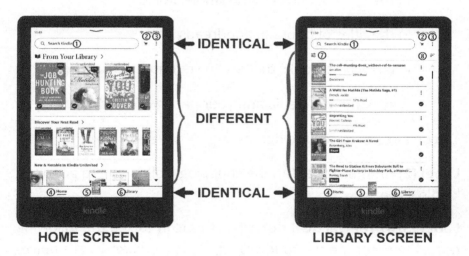

HOME SCREEN   **LIBRARY SCREEN**

Figure 4-1: The Home screen and Library screen.
The labels are described below. You can download this figure from ianallanauthor.com/paperwhite.

Your paperwhite's *Home* screen and *Library* screen are broken into three sections (Figure 4-1). Their top and their bottom are identical. The bit in the middle is different. The *Home* screen is mostly a kindle store that has been curated for you based on what amazon knows about your reading preferences. The *Library* screen displays all your books, some or all of which will have already downloaded to your paperwhite. Other books might still be in the cloud, so you may need to tap on their thumbnails to force them to download.

In Figure 4-1, the top menu bar contains. . .

Label (1) Search bar: Type a term into the search bar and amazon searches for it . . .

- In the titles of books within your library.

- In the titles of books in the kindle store.

- In the titles of books in goodreads.

- Inside all the books that are in your library.

- And within Wikipedia and your paperwhite's dictionary.

Tap on a result to see the details.

Label (2) Kindle store: Tap the shopping trolley icon to go to the kindle store.

Label (3) Three vertical dots: Tap this icon to see the following tappable menu items. *Your Reading Lists (samples you've down-loaded), Goodreads, Web Browser, Settings, Legal, and Create a Collection*.

The bottom menu bar has links to. . .

Label (4) The *Home* screen.

Label (5) The book that you're currently reading.

Label (6) The *Library* screen.

The Home Screen

The Home screen has two types of thumbnails...

- **Thumbnails in the *From Your Library* area:** These are books that you have recently opened.

- **Thumbnails in the *Recommendations* area:** This is a curated version of the kindle store that has been personalized for you. There's groups of thumbnails that are designed to help you choose your next book. Each group contains personalized book recommendations based on your reading history, search history and preferences. Tap on a heading to expand the recommendations. Depending on the popularity of the category, there might be just a few, or up to 99. I like to read widely so I often check the amazon app and amazon store for recommendations as well. You'll get even broader recommendations if you log out of the amazon store and search it from a browser that's in private mode.

The Library Screen

The *Library* screen is where you access and manage all of the books and other content that you have purchased or downloaded onto your paperwhite. Just above the book thumbnails, there's a *Filter* icon and a *Sort by / View options* icon.

The *Filter* icon: The *Filter* icon (label (7) in Figure 4-1) is on the left near the top of the *Library* screen. From here you can choose to *Filter* your library content by a combination of. . ..

- **Status:** Downloaded, unread, read.

- **Program:** Kindle Unlimited, Prime, Audible, Comixology.

- **Type:** Book, sample, document, newsstand, comic, collection.

***The Sort by* and *View options* icon:** The *Sort by* and *View options* icon (label (8) in Figure 4-1) is on the right near the top of the *Library* screen.

- **The Sort by option:** You can sort your Library content by a combination of. . .

  ○ Most recently read, title, author, or publication date.

  ○ Ascending or descending.

- **The View options:** You can choose to display your content as either a grid or a list. The title and cover thumbnail of each item is displayed.

  ○ **View as a Grid:** When displayed as a grid, the top-right corner of each thumbnail has information about your relationship to the book – "Read", "Sample", and Percentage progress eg. "50% complete". The bottom left corner shows the relationship between the book and your paperwhite - a tick means that it's downloaded. If the book is one of a series, a number on the thumbnail indicates how many of the series you have on your paperwhite. Or, if it's a collection you're looking at, a number on the thumbnail indicates how many books there are in the collection.

  ○ **View as a List:** When displayed as a list, the area under the author name has information about your relationship to the book – "Read", "Sample", Percentage progress eg. "50% complete". The bottom right corner of the book's row shows the relationship between the book and your paperwhite - a tick means that it's down-loaded.

- **View Collections:** You can also choose to display your collections. I talk about collections in Chapter 7.

In any of the views, you tap on a thumbnail to open it. Sometimes your tap will trigger a book to download from the cloud first. If you tap-and-hold on a thumbnail, or tap the three vertical dots to the right of a thumbnail, you'll launch the book's options menu. There's a bunch of things you can do in there - delete it, add it to a collection, view it in the Kindle Store, and more.

4.3 - How to read a Book

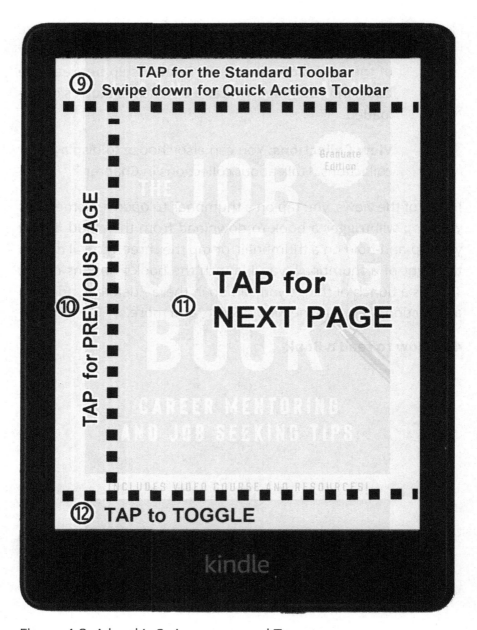

Figure 4-2: A book's Swipe zones and Tap zones.
The labels are described below. You can download this figure from ianallanauthor.com/paperwhite.

Swipe down from the top of the screen to see the Quick actions toolbar (Figure 4-3). Tap the top of the screen to see the Standard toolbar (Figure 4-4). Tap on the left side of the screen for the previous page, and the right side of the screen for the next page. Tap the bottom left of the screen to toggle through your reading progress information. You can download this figure from ianallanauthor.com/paperwhite.

Tapping a book's thumbnail – that's any thumbnail in your *Library*, or the book icon at the bottom of your *Home screen* and your *Library* screen (label (5) in Figure 4-1), opens the book and takes you to the last page you read in that book. In an open book, there's TAP zones and SWIPE zones. These are labelled in Figure 4-2. . .

Label (9): Swipe down from the top of the screen and the *Quick Actions* toolbar will appear (Figure 4-3). Tap at the top of the screen and the Standard toolbar will appear (Figure 4-4).

Label (10): Tap on the left of the screen and return to the previous page.

Label (11): Tap on the right of the screen and advance to the next page.

Label (12): Tap the bottom-left of the screen and toggle between the following reading progress options – page number, time left in chapter, time left in book, location, and blank.

4.4 - How to read a Graphic Novel

To read a graphic novel you'll need to adopt a slightly different reading technique. Graphic novels have *panel view* and *frame view* options.

- **Panel view:** The *panel view* is a whole comic book page from where you can tap on the right for the next page or tap on the left for the previous page (see label (10) and label (11) in Figure 4-2).

- **Frame view:** If you double-tap on a frame in a panel view, the frame will enlarge to be full-screen. You can then progress through the comic frame-by-frame by single-tapping on the right to advance to the next frame, or on the left to return to the previous frame (see label (10) and label (11) in Figure 4-2).

4.5 - How to Zoom and Pan on an Image

You can zoom and pan on an image:

- **To enlarge an image:** Tap-and-hold on the image. Then tap the magnifying glass that appears, and the image will enlarge.

- **Zoom in or out on an image:** Spread two fingers apart to zoom in, or pinch two fingers together to zoom out.

- **Pan an image:** To pan an image, swipe your finger across the screen in the direction you want to move it.

4.6 – The Quick Actions toolbar
Book > swipe down from top for the Quick Actions toolbar

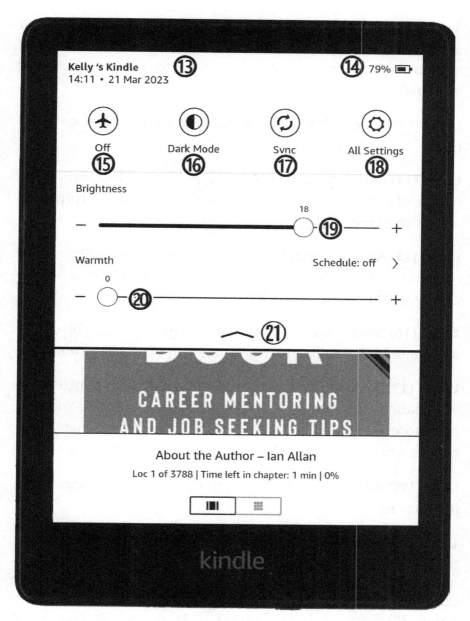

Figure 4-3: The Quick actions toolbar.
The labels are described below. You can download this figure from ianallanauthor.com/paperwhite.

Swipe down from the top of any screen (*Home, Library,* or in a Book) to access the *Quick Actions* toolbar. The icons in Figure 4-3 are labeled so that they are easy to refer to. There's a bunch of information and tools in here. . .

Label (13) General information: Name of kindle device, date and time.

Label (14) Percentage charged: A lightening bold appears in the middle of the battery symbol when your paperwhite is turned on and its charging.

Label (15) Airplane mode: Tap the icon to toggle airplane mode on and off. Airplane mode can also extend the life of a battery charge because it turns off Wi-Fi.

Label (16) Dark mode: Tap the icon to toggle between black text and white background, and white text with black background.

Label (17) Synchronize: Tap the icon to manually synchronize your paperwhite with all your kindle apps and devices. You may need to use this if your paperwhite hasn't detected that you've bought a book from the kindle store on a different device.

Label (18) All settings: Tap the icon to access the *Settings* menu (Chapter 8).

Label (19) Screen brightness slider: Tap and hold the slider, or tap the + or the − symbols for brightness values ranging from 0 to 24.

Label (20) Warmth slider: Tap and hold the slider, or tap the + or the − symbols for warmth values ranging from 0 to 24.

Label (21) Up arrow: Tap the up arrow to minimize the *Quick* *access* menu.

4.7 - The Standard toolbar

Book > tap top for Standard toolbar

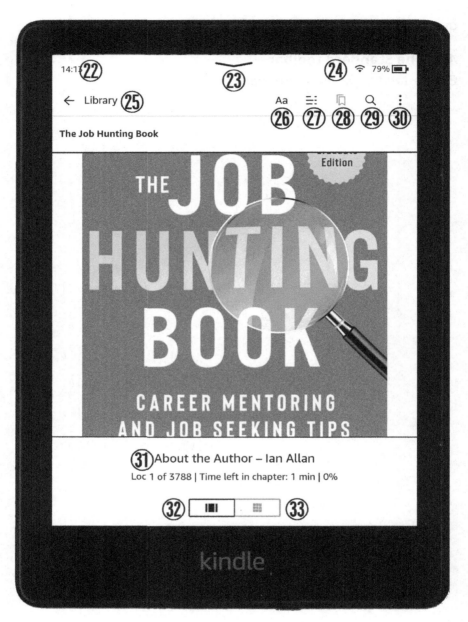

Figure 4-4: The Standard Toolbar.
The labels are explained below. You can download this figure from ianallanauthor.com/paperwhite.

Tap the top of the screen to access the *Standard* toolbar. There's a bunch of information in here, and there's also tools to turbo-charge your paperwhite experience. Like Figure 4-3, Figure 4-4 is labeled so that the screen capture is easier to refer to. If you are new to the paperwhite, the most useful item in this toolbar is likely to be the *Display Settings* icon (label (26) in Figure 4-4 and all of Chapter 6).

Label (22) Time: You set the time in the *Settings* menu (Chapter 8). It's a 12 hour clock in a Gen-10 paperwhite and a 24 hour clock in a Gen-11 paperwhite.

Label (23) *Quick Actions* toolbar: Swipe down on the arrow to launch the *Quick Actions* toolbar (Figure 4-3).

Label (24) Wi-Fi signal strength (and % charged): On most paperwhites this will be Wi-Fi strength. On some gen 10 models it will be a 4g signal strength. The percentage figure indicates how much charge your paperwhite has.

Label (25) Return arrow: Tap the arrow to return to whichever one of the *Home* or *Library* screens you were last at.

Label (26) Display Settings: Tap this icon to access the *Themes*, *Font*, *Layout*, and *More* menus (Chapter 6).

Label (27) Contents, notes and highlights: Tap the icon to be taken to the book's table of contents page and Notes and Highlights page (Chapter 5).

Label (28) Bookmarks: Tap the icon to manage your *Bookmarks* (Chapter 5).

Label (29) Search: Tap this icon to launch the *search* bar and keypad. You can search for a word in your book, and in your notes and highlights.

Label (30) 3 vertical dots: Tap this icon for additional options – information about the book, the notes and highlights box (also accessed from Label (27)), X-Ray and Vocabulary builder (Chapter 5), the *Settings* menu (Chapter 8), and more.

Label (31) Reading progress: This area displays information about your reading progress, where you are in the book, and how much of the book you have read.

The Pageflip toolbar allows you to preview a different page in a book without losing your place.

Label (32) Pageview: Tap this to display Pageflip as a single page.

Label (33) Grid view: Tap this to display Pageflip as a 9 page grid.

Tap the X in the top right corner of the box to return to your book.

4.8 - The kindle store

Your Paperwhite is part of the Amazon ecosystem. It is linked to your amazon account, and the massive Kindle Store that contains millions of titles, including bestsellers, new releases, and classic literature.

Due to the royalty sharing arrangements with authors (books less than $10 attract double the royalty), Kindle books are often a fraction of the cost of their hardcopy cousins, and they're available near-instantly.

In this section I'll show you how to use the kindle store from your paperwhite. You can access it from. . ..

- The curated kindle store on your *Home* screen (Figure 4-1).

- The shopping cart button on your *Home* screen and your *Library* screen (label (2) in Figure 4-1).

- The search bar on your *Home* screen and your *Library* screen (label (1) in Figure 4-1).

There's other ways to buy and send books to your paperwhite too. I talk about those in Chapter 7.

Kindle Store from the Home Screen

The *Home* screen (Figure 4-1), is a version of the kindle store that's customized to you. It's divided into categories like *From your Library*, *Kindle Unlimited Recommendations*, *Similar to your last* read, etc. Tap the > symbol next to a heading and it will expand to a list of tappable book thumbnails and titles.

Tap a book thumbnail and you'll be taken to its sales page in the kindle store.

Kindle Store from the Shopping Cart icon
Home | Library > shopping cart

From the *Home* screen or *Library* screen, tap the shopping cart icon (label (2) in Figure 4-1) to open the Kindle Store. You'll be taken to a screen that looks similar to the *Home* screen, except that it has more options.

You'll see *featured* categories like *Prime Reading* and *Kindle Unlimited* (Chapter 10). And under each of these categories, sub-categories like *nonfiction, romance* and *graphics novels.*

You can refine your search by categories, or scroll through the categories and books that Amazon recommends to you, based on your search and purchasing history. Tap the *See more* ▶ label next to the category name to expand it into a scrollable view.

Kindle Store from the Search Bar

Home | Library > Search Kindle

From the *Home* screen or *Library* screen, tap in the *Search Kindle* box (label (1) in Figure 4-1), and use the keyboard that appears to type in the name of a book, author, or topic, and Amazon will display a list of matching results from the Kindle store, as well as titles in your *Library*, goodreads, within books in your library, and the dictionary and Wikipedia.

Book sales page

Tap on a book thumbnail to open its sales page in the kindle store. There you can read its description, reviews, download sample pages, and buy it (chapter 7). Or, if you're a Prime member or Kindle Unlimited subscriber, you could borrow an eligible book (chapter 9).

4.9 - How to Bookmark a Page

Book > Tap top for Standard toolbar > Bookmark icon > ⊕ icon

To manage bookmarks on your Paperwhite, while reading a book, tap the top of your screen to show the *Standard* toolbar, then tap the *Bookmark* icon (label (28) in Figure 4-4). Or, tap the top-right corner of the screen. An options box will appear so you can. . .

- **Add a bookmark:** Tap the ⊕ icon.

- **Delete a bookmark:** From the list of bookmarked pages, tap the bookmark, and then the ⊟ that appears next to it.

- **View your bookmarks:** A list of all your bookmarks and their page numbers are displayed. Tap the bookmark you want to go to.

4.10 - Find a Page or Location

Book > tap top for Standard toolbar > Contents | Notes & Highlights icon > Page or Location.

To go to a page or a location while you're reading a book, tap the top of your screen to show the *Standard* toolbar, then tap the *Contents* icon (label (27) in Figure 4-4). Then tap the *Page or Location* item in the *Contents* box. In the box that launches, enter a page number or location number to be taken there.

Kindle books are reflowable text. That's text that you can adjust to suit your reading preferences (Chapter 6). Reflowable text makes the page numbers displayed on your paperwhite are unreliable and they may not match the book's printed version. So, if you need to formally reference an eBook, you should consider referencing a location number as well as a page number.

4.11 - Table of Contents

Book > tap top for Standard toolbar > Contents | Notes & Highlights icon

To show a book's table of contents, while reading a book, tap the top of your screen to show the *Standard* toolbar, then tap the *Contents* icon (label (27) in Figure 4-4). Then tap on a chapter to be taken there.

Chapter 5

Your paperwhite as a learning aid

In a book, tap, hold and release to select a word, phrase or passage, and a world of possibilities open up. You can highlight, annotate, note take, translate, look up a dictionary, and improve your vocabulary. Sorry, I couldn't resist rhyming that!

5.1 - Quickstart

Tap and hold on a word or passage to launch a menu bar, a box, or depending on context, both.

- *Tap, hold and release on a word and a box will launch with Dictionary, Wikipedia and Translation options.*

- *Tap, hold and release on a noun and the X-Ray box appears.*

- *Drag your finger and select a word or phrase to Highlight it, write a Note about, Share it or Search for it throughout the book you're reading, every book in your Library, or the kindle store. Depending on what you select, the Thesaurus, Dictionary or Translation box will also launch.*

- *Tap a highlighted passage to Delete the highlight.*

- *Tap the top of the screen to display the Standard toolbar.*

Then tap the ⋮ *icon to launch the Vocabulary Builder. You use that to test your knowledge of words that you've looked up in your paperwhite's dictionary.*

5.2 - Dictionary

Book > tap, hold and release on a word > Dictionary

In a book, tap, hold and release on a word and a box will appear with its definition. I use this feature all the time. It's nothing short of amazing. For most words, information like part-of-speech, pronunciation, and usage examples are also included.

Tap the dictionary name at the bottom right corner of the box and another box appears. From here you can choose to use a different *installed* dictionary. My Paperwhite has *the Oxford dictionary of English* and *the new Oxford American dictionary* installed. You can install any number of the 50+ other dictionaries from your amazon account in a web browser (Chapter 9).

Tap outside the box to close it and return to your book.

5.3 - Wikipedia

Book > tap, hold and release on a word or phrase > swipe > Wikipedia

In a book, tap, hold and release on a word or phrase, and the dictionary box will appear. Choose *Wikipedia* from the dropdown list in the top left corner of the dictionary box, or swipe left.

Tap outside the box to close it and return to your book.

5.4 - Translation

Your Paperwhite can translate between many languages – according to threads on forums, with varying levels of success. You can translate a word or phrase, or a passage of text.

Translate a Word or Phrase

Book > tap and hold on a word or phrase > swipe > swipe > Translation

In a book, tap, hold and release on a word or phrase, and the *Dictionary* box will appear. Choose *Translation* from the dropdown list in the top left corner of the dictionary box, or swipe left twice. Select the *From* and *To* languages from the drop-down lists, and the translation will be displayed.

Tap outside the box to close it and return to your book.

Translate a Passage

Book > tap and drag on a passage >⋮ > Translation

In a book, tap, hold and release on a passage. Tap the ⋮ icon in the toolbar that appears, and then *Translation*. Select the *From* and *To* languages from the drop-down lists and the translation will be displayed.

Tap outside the box to close it and return to your book.

5.5 - X-Ray

X-Ray lets you find extra information about the characters, places, and terms mentioned in a book. You can use X-Ray to see the first mention of a selection – I talk about that option under the *single item* heading below. Or you can use X-Ray to see every mention of a selection in your book – I talk about that option under the *all items* heading below.

Not all books have this functionality. But when they do, it's magic. Especially if your memory for names and places is as bad as mine! Check for *X-Ray enabled* on the book's sale page. Otherwise, tap the ⋮ icon in the *Standard* Toolbar (label   in Figure 44). The X-Ray menu item will be greyed out if it's unavailable.

X-Ray is a really useful tool. Armed with the brief overview I'm about to give you, I encourage you to take the time to explore it.

X-Ray - Single items
Book > Tap and hold on a word

Tap and hold to select a place name or character name and the X-Ray box will appear. It shows you the sentence containing the first time the selection is mentioned in your book.

X-Ray - All items
Book > tap and hold on a word > Open X-Ray

Tap and hold a place name or character name to select it and the X-Ray box will appear. Tap *Open X-Ray* in the bottom right corner of the box to launch another box that has your selection as its title. The box has a *notable clips* tab and an *all mentions* tab.

- **The *Notable clips* tab:** The *Notable Clips* tab is where you can view passages relating to your selection that other readers have highlighted. *Notable Clips* are common in popular books. The tab has a bar with a marker underneath indicating your current place in the book. That's so you can avoid looking ahead and finding *spoilers*. There's scrolling functionality for long clips, and small (hard-to-see) *next* and *previous* mention arrows.

- **The *All mentions* tab:** The *All Mentions* tab is where you can see every mention of your selection in the book, and a tappable link to each mention.

X-Ray – From the ⋮ icon
Book > ⋮ > X-Ray

While reading a book, tap the top of your screen to show the

Standard toolbar, then tap the ⋮ icon (label (30) in Figure 4-4). From this menu, tap X-Ray, and in the menu that appears, you'll see tabs for *Notable Clips*, *People*, *Terms*, and *Images.* In each tab, items are noted by name, and the number of times that they are mentioned. The results can be sorted according to their relevance, or alphabetically. Tap any item to be taken to that place in your book.

5.6 - Highlight a passage
Book > tap, hold and release on a word or passage > highlight

While reading a book, tap, hold and release on a word or passage. An *Options* box will launch. Tap outside the box and the selection will be highlighted.

Any passages you highlight get saved to your Amazon account in the cloud. You can access them from the Notes & Highlights menu (label (27) in Figure 4-4). If it's a Kindle Unlimited book that you've returned, your highlights will be reinstated if you borrow the book again.

You can also view your *Highlights* in the kindle cloud reader (Chapter 9), without having to borrow the book again.

You can also color code your highlights in the kindle cloud reader, and in the kindle apps on your desktop or smart device.

5.7 - Adding notes
Book > tap, hold and release on a word or passage > Note

To add a note, tap, hold and release on a word or passage, and in the box that appears, tap *Note*. Use the keyboard that appears to enter your note and then tap the *Save* button. The text will be highlighted and a note number added as a superscript following the text that you selected.

All notes are saved to your Amazon account in the cloud. You can access them from the *Notes & Highlights* menu (label (27) in Figure 4-4). If it's a Kindle Unlimited book that you've returned, your notes will still be there if you borrow the book again. You can view your *Notes* in the kindle cloud reader (Chapter 9) without having to borrow the book again.

Adding notes on your paperwhite can be a bit clunky, but you can revise them in any kindle app (eg. on your desktop) or in the kindle cloud reader in your browser (Chapter 9).

To delete a note, tap the note's superscript, and then the *Delete* button in the box that appears.

Sharing notes and highlighted passages
Book > tap on a highlighted word or passage >   OR Book > tap top for Standard toolbar > Notes & Highlights (label (27) in Figure 4-4)

Because each Kindle device has its own email address, you can share passages that you highlighted. Your Paperwhite sends your highlighted text along with a reference to the book. Here's an example of a highlighted passage that I shared to my personal email.

> *"Stacey pushed aside any rule she didn't consider worthy of following." (from "The Decoy: A Riveting Espionage Suspense Thriller . . ." by Chloé Archambault)*

Within the sharing box, you can share to an email address or to your goodreads account.

- **Email:** Tap the email button and a prefilled (editable) email box displays. By default, the email includes your highlight as a quote, as well as a link to the book in the amazon store. Enter an email address using the keyboard that appears, and then tap "send".

- **Goodreads:** Tap the goodreads button and a prefilled (editable) message box displays with your highlight as a quote, as well as a preview of the book. You can add an extra note if you want to. Tap *Share* to post.

Sharing a reference to the book you're reading
Book > tap top for Standard toolbar > ⋮ > Settings > Share

This sharing option allows you to share a reference to the book you're reading directly to someone's email address or to goodreads. To use the sharing option:

- While reading your book, tap the top of the screen to show the *Standard* toolbar, then tap the ⋮ icon (label (30) in Figure 4-4). From the menu that appears, tap *Share*.

- Then select the sharing method. . .

  ◦ **Email:** A prefilled (editable) email box displays. The message contains the full reference for the book, and a link to it in the Amazon store. Enter an email address using the keyboard that appears, and then tap the *Send* button.
  ◦ **Goodreads:** Share the book and your reading progress to your goodreads account. Add a note if you want. Tap the *Share* button to post.

Export notes

Book > Tap top for Standard toolbar > Notes and Highlights > Export Notes

From the *Notes and Highlights* menu (label (27) in in Figure 4-4), tap the *Export* button to have all the notes from your book sent to the email address that's attached to your Amazon account. You cannot export individual notes.

5.8 - Vocabulary Builder

Book > Tap top for Standard Toolbar > ⋮ > Vocabulary Builder

The vocabulary builder records words that you've looked up in the dictionary, and presents them as a grid for you to study and master. It's a great tool to help you remember words, and to improve your vocabulary and reading comprehension. I imagine that it would be incredibly useful to language learners.

You can toggle to show a list of all *Words* that you've looked up, or according to the *Book* you looked the word up in. When you tap on a word, a box displays its definition.

There's also an option to show flashcards of random words from the list. Tap the *Flashcards* label at the bottom of the vocabulary builder to access this. The flashcard displays the word in a sentence from the book you looked it up in, and optionally, its definition too.

Each word is flagged as being one that you're either *Learning* or have *Mastered*. There's a 2000 word limit. When you reach that limit you can delete words to make room for more.

Chapter 6

The Display Settings box

Book > Tap top for the Standard Toolbar > Aa

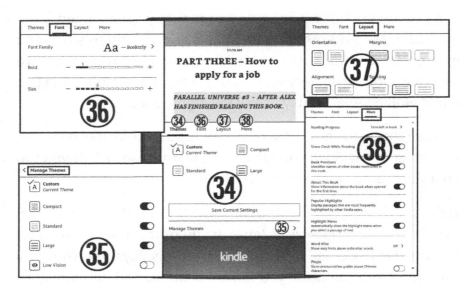

Figure 6-1: Tap the Aa icon in the Standard Toolbar to launch the Display Settings box.

The labels are explained below. In the figure, the small numbers next to the menu items match the large numbers in the boxes. You can download this figure from ianallanauthor.com/paperwhite.

Your paperwhite uses a special format called reflowable text. It is similar to text editors like MS Word in that you have lots of ways to customize how a document looks on your screen. That's what this chapter is about – taking advantage of reflowable text to customize the way your books look on your paperwhite.

While reading a book, tap the top of the screen to reveal the *Standard* toolbar. Then tap the Aa icon (label (26) in Figure 4-4). The box that appears contains four submenus - *Themes*, *Font*, *Layout*, and *More*. The changes you make in these menus apply to your current book and all subsequent books that you open.

6.1 - The *Themes* sub-menu

Book > Tap top for the Standard Toolbar > Aa > Themes

To display the *Themes* sub-menu, while reading a book, tap the top of the screen to reveal the *Standard* toolbar. Then tap the Aa icon, and then *Themes* (label (34) in Figure 6-1).

Themes are a mix of font size, style, and line spacing that you customize to suit your reading preferences. There are three default settings to experiment with (compact, standard and large). There's also a *Low Vision* theme in the *Manage Themes* box (label (35) in Figure 6-1). You can create a custom theme by making changes in the sub-menus, and then tapping the *Save Current Settings* button.

6.2 - The *Font* sub-menu

Book > Tap top for the Standard Toolbar > Aa > Font

To display the *Font* sub-menu, while reading a book, tap the top of the screen to reveal the *Standard* toolbar. Then tap the Aa icon, and then on *Font* (label (36) in Figure 6-1).

You can change the font family (there's 9 fonts) and text size to suit your reading preferences, and preview your changes in real-time before applying them. . .

- Use the sliders to adjust the text boldness and text size. There are 5 levels of bold and 14 font sizes.

- Tap on the font name to choose a different font.

- After adjusting the font and text size, tap outside the box to save your changes and return to your book.

- You can also adjust the text size by using a pinching action with two fingers.

This functionality only applies to books with reflowable text (eg. ePub). You cannot change the text size in your paperwhite's menus or in pdf documents.

6.3 - The *Layout* sub-menu
Book > Tap top for the Standard Toolbar > Aa > Layout

To display the *Layout* sub-menu, while reading a book, tap the top of the screen to reveal the *Standard* toolbar. Then tap the Aa icon, and then *Layout* (label (37) in Figure 6-1).

You can customize orientation, margins, text alignment and line spacing. . .

- **Orientation:** Choose portrait or landscape.

- **Margins:** Adjust the amount of white space around the edges of the text on the screen.

- **Text alignment:** Choose whether the text is aligned to the left, or justified.

- **Line spacing:** Adjust the amount of space between lines of text on the screen.

6.4 - The *More* sub-menu (additional features)

Book > Tap top for the Standard Toolbar > Aa > More

To display the *More* sub-menu, while reading a book, tap the top of the screen to reveal the *Standard* toolbar. Then tap the Aa icon, and then on *More* (label (38) in Figure 6-1).

This menu provides access to additional options for customizing your reading experience. They include *Reading Progress, Show clock while reading, Book mentions, About this book, Popular highlights, Highlights menu,* and *Word Wise*.

Reading Progress

Book > Tap top for the Standard Toolbar > Aa > More > Reading Progress

To display the *Reading Progress* option, while reading a book, tap the top of the screen to reveal the *Standard* toolbar. Then tap the Aa icon, and then on *More* (label (38) in Figure 6-1), then on *Reading Progress*.

This option lets you control the text that displays in the bottom left corner of your screen. The options include *Page in book, Time left in chapter, Time left in book, Location in book,* and *None*.

While you're reading a book, you can also tap the text in the bottom-left corner and advance through the options.

Show clock while reading

Book > Tap top for the Standard Toolbar > Aa > More > Show clock while reading

To display the *Show clock while reading* option, while reading a book, tap the top of the screen to reveal the *Standard* toolbar. Then tap the Aa icon, and then on *More* (label (38) in Figure 6-1), then on *Show clock while reading*.

The clock displays at the top of the screen while you're reading. This option lets you toggle the clock on and off. You set the clock time in the *Settings* menu (Chapter 8).

Book mentions

Book > Tap top for the Standard Toolbar > Aa > More > Book mentions

To display the *Book mentions* option, while reading a book, tap the top of the screen to reveal the *Standard* toolbar. Then tap the Aa icon, and then on *More* (label (38) in Figure 6-1), then on *Book mentions*.

Where an author mentions another book, toggling this option on lets you tap on the book mention and be taken to the book in the kindle store. To be honest, I've not had much luck with this.

About this book

Book > Tap top for the Standard Toolbar > Aa > More > About this book

To display the *About this book* option, while reading a book, tap the top of the screen to reveal the *Standard* toolbar. Then tap the Aa icon, and then on *More* (label (38) in Figure 6-1), then on *About this book*.

When you open a book for the first time, a box appears showing you some general information about the book (eg. popular highlights, more by this author, etc), as well as giving you the option to *Mark as currently reading* in goodreads. Toggle to enable or disable this functionality.

Popular highlights

Book > Tap top for the Standard Toolbar > Aa > More > Popular highlights

To display the *Popular highlights* option, while reading a book, tap the top of the screen to reveal the *Standard* toolbar. Then tap the Aa icon, and then on *More* (label (38) in Figure 6-1), then on *Popular highlights*.

Toggle this on to display passages that have been highlighted by other readers. *Popular highlights* appear with a fine dotted underline, and small text saying eg. "578 highlighters". The useful thing about this functionality is that, well, maybe a passage that's been highlighted by 578 people is one that you should pay greater attention to?

Highlights menu

Book > Tap top for the Standard Toolbar > Aa > More > Highlights menu

To display the *Highlights menu* option, while reading a book, tap the top of the screen to reveal the *Standard* toolbar. Then tap the Aa icon, and then on *More* (label (38) in Figure 6-1), then on *Highlights menu*.

Toggle this on and off. This menu is important if you like to take notes. When you highlight a piece of text. . .

- If the *highlights* menu is toggled on, a menu appears asking you if you want to highlight it and make a note about it.

- If the *highlights* menu is toggled off, the text is highlighted, and no note taking menu appears.

Word Wise

Book > Tap top of screen for the Standard toolbar > Aa > More > Word Wise

To display the *Word Wise* option, while reading a book, tap the top of the screen to reveal the *Standard* toolbar. Then tap the Aa icon, and then on *More* (label (38) in Figure 6-1), then on *Word Wise*.

This menu option lets you toggle *Word Wise* on and off, and adjust the level of help it provides.

Word Wise provides short above-text definitions for challenging words. The lines in your book become double-spaced to make room for the definitions to display in a tiny font above the word. You can also tap on a word that *Word Wise* recognizes and a box will launch with a more detailed definition.

Personally, I find *Word Wise* to be distracting, but I imagine that it would be incredibly useful to language learners.

Could you spare a moment to review my book?

Don't forget the resources page at ianallanauthor.com/paperwhite

I would be so grateful if you would leave a review on Amazon. . .

Chapter 7

Acquiring and managing content

In this chapter I'll show you how to add books and other types of files to your Paperwhite from your paperwhite's kindle store, and sources such as the kindle app, the amazon app, and the amazon website. I'll also show you how to transfer files from your computer using drag-and-drop from a web browser, as an email attachment, and directly using the cable that came with your paperwhite. Finally, I'll show you how to send a web page to your paperwhite, and how to organize your content into collections.

7.1 - Quickstart

- *Tap on a thumbnail in the Home screen to be taken to a book's sales page.*

- *Tap on the shopping cart icon in the Home screen to be taken to the kindle store.*

- *Tap on the Buy button on a sales page to buy a kindle book.*

- *Kindle Unlimited subscribers and Prime members can tap the read now for $0.00 button to borrow an eligible book.*

- *Add a non-amazon book to your paperwhite using the*

drag-and-drop amazon.com/sendtokindle web page.

- *Share a webpage to your paperwhite using Share on your smartphone, or the Send To Kindle chrome extension on your desktop.*

7.2 - How to transfer content from your computer to your paperwhite

You can transfer a book or file from your computer to your paperwhite using the sendtokindle web page, as an email attachment, or directly via a cable. The simplest and most reliable method is the amazon.com/SendToKindle drag-and-drop web page, followed by sending a file as an email attachment.

SendtoKindle and emailing a file attachment overcome a bunch of the problems that you're likely to have if you use cable transfer. Often your paperwhite won't recognize a cable-transferred file, but will recognize the same file if its sent via the amazon cloud. That's because the Amazon cloud checks your file for compatibility, rejects incompatible file types, sometimes mends incompatible files, and places the book or file onto your paperwhite using Amazon's folder structure standards.

You can transfer twelve file types to your Paperwhite - .azw, .epub, .mobi, .pdf, .doc, .docx, .rtf, and .html document files. Also .png, .jpg, .gif and .bmp image files.

You can also send a web page to your paperwhite using *Send* on your smartphone, or the *Send To Kindle* extension for google chrome. This is a great way to read newspapers on your paperwhite.

Now let's look more closely at these computer-to-paperwhite file transfer techniques.

SendToKindle drag-and-drop transfer
Amazon.com/sendtokindle

SendToKindle is the most simple and reliable way to transfer a book from your computer to your paperwhite. Log into your amazon account and go to *amazon.com/sendtokindle*. From here you can drag-and-drop any kindle compatible file into your kindle cloud and it will be available on all your kindle devices, including your paperwhite. The sendtokindle page has a status area showing that the file is *Processing*, and that it is *In [your] Library* when the transfer is successful.

Email transfer
⋮ > *Settings > Your Account > Send-to-Kindle email*

OR

Amazon in a web browser > Accounts & Lists drop-down menu > Manage content and devices > Devices > Amazon apps installed on devices > Kindle (now pick your paperwhite from the list).

To email a book from your computer to your Paperwhite . . .

1. **You will need to send it to your paperwhite's email address:** Here's where you find that. . .

   - **To find the email address on your paperwhite:** Tap the top of the screen for the *Standard* toolbar, then tap ⋮ , *then Settings,* then *Your Account and* then *Send-to-Kindle email.*

   - **To find the email address in a web browser:** From your local amazon web page, click *Your account,* then

Manage content and devices, then *Devices,* then *Amazon apps installed on devices,* then *Kindle (and pick your paperwhite from the list).*

Pay attention when you're copying the email address. Unfortunately, kindle email addresses often contain both the number zero and the letter O, and they look near-identical. If you look closely (or maybe take a photo on your smartphone so you can enlarge it), the letter O is more circular and the number zero is more egg shaped (O the letter versus 0 the number).

2. **You need to send the file from an approved email address:** For security reasons, the email address you're sending from must be on your *approved personal document email list.* I talk about that later in this chapter.

3. **You can only send supported file types:** Only file types that are supported by Kindle will be delivered to your device. I mentioned those file types in the introduction to this section.

With those three things in place (ie. your paperwhite's email address, an approved from-email address, and compatible file type), you can now send a file as an attachment to your paperwhite's email address. The file will be checked and processed by Amazon, and then delivered to your paperwhite. Be patient. Although most times you'll only need to wait a minute or two, files can sometimes take up to 15 minutes to appear in your library.

As an aside, pdf files keep their format when you transfer them to your paperwhite. This means that you can't adjust the way that a pdf displays on your screen. However, if you email a pdf file with the word "convert" in the subject line, amazon will convert it into kindle format as a part of the transfer.

Cable transfer

Transfer books from your computer to your Paperwhite using the USB cable that came with it.

Connect the cable to your computer, and your paperwhite will appear in your computer's file manager as a removable disk. You can drag-and-drop, or copy-and-paste your files to your paperwhite as you would to any external disk. There are two ways to setup the transfer. . .

1. Copy the file from your computer to your Paperwhite's *documents* folder. For me, this only worked for pdf files.

2. Create a folder called the name of your file in your paperwhites *documents* folder and copy your file there. So, for a book called today.epub, you would create a folder called "today" in your paperwhites *documents* folder, and then add today.epub to the folder.

After transferring a book, eject your Paperwhite from your computer and the book will appear in your *Library*.

I advise against using the cable transfer technique unless you have no other option. Too frequently, this technique comes with the unwanted bonus of frustration and swearing. I also found that it can lead to excessive alcohol consumption!

Send a web page from your desktop using Chrome.

On your desktop, in the Chrome browser, google "send to kindle chrome extension". Click on the link to the Chrome store and then the *add to desktop* button. Once the extension is installed. . .

- Login to your amazon account.

- In a webpage, tap the "K" button that the extension added to your browser toolbar. That will open the *Send To Kindle* dialog box.

- In the settings menu, choose your paperwhite as the kindle device that you want to send to.

- Click *Send To Kindle* and the web page will be sent to your kindle. Allow a minute or two for it to appear in your *Library*.

Send a web page from your smart phone.

You can send a web page to your paperwhite from your smartphone or other smart device.

- Add your email to your paperwhite's approved email address list (see below).

- In a web page, tap the share button and *Kindle* as the app to share with. You may also need to have the kindle app installed on your device and connected to your account for this share option to appear.

Manage your paperwhite's email address

Amazon in a web browser > Accounts & Lists drop-down menu > Manage your content and devices > Preferences > Personal document settings > . . .

You can change your paperwhite's email address if you don't like the one that amazon assigned to it. Also, if you plan to email a file to your paperwhite, you'll need to add the address that you'll be emailing from to your paperwhite's approved email-from-addresses. You manage these email addresses in the *Personal document settings* area of your amazon account. From your local amazon web page, click *Your account,* then *Manage your content and devices,* then *Preferences,* then *Personal document settings. . .*

- **To change your paperwhite's email address:** Every one of your kindle devices (Kindle apps and other kindle devices) has its own email address. Click the edit button next to the *Send-to-Kindle email* to change your paperwhite's email address. You should make it a hard-for-spammers-to-guess email address. Otherwise you may find that amazon starts to send you validation emails every time you, or a spammer, sends an email to your paperwhite.

- **Approved Personal Document E-mail List:** Your paperwhite can only accept emails (and attachments) from addresses that are listed on your account as approved *send-from* email addresses. Click the *Add a new approved e-mail address* link in the *Approved Personal Document E-mail List* area and add the email address that you'll be sending your files from.

7.3 - How to sample, buy or borrow a book

Tap on a book thumbnail on your paperwhite, in the kindle app, or in the amazon store in a web browser and you'll be taken to its sales page. There you can download a sample of the book, buy it, or borrow it if it's an eligible book and you're a Prime member or Kindle Unlimited subscriber.

How to sample a book

On a book's sales page, tap *Try a sample* to download, usually 10% of the book. The sample will show up in your *Library*. Tap the thumbnail to read it, and on the sample's last page Amazon will give you the option to buy it.

You can delete a sample by tapping and holding on the book thumbnail and then tapping on *Remove this sample* in the menu that appears.

How to buy a book from your paperwhite

To buy a book, tap on a thumbnail in the *Home* screen or from the kindle store that launches from the Shopping Cart icon (label (2) in Figure 4-1), and you'll be taken to the book's sales page in the kindle store. When you tap the *Buy* button on the book's sales page, the book will automatically download to your paperwhite and be processed using the payment method associated with your Amazon account.

How to buy a book from a web browser

Once you're signed into Amazon on your browser, find a kindle book and tap the button that sometimes reads *Buy now with 1 click* and other times *read for $0.00*. The book will be delivered to your paperwhite, and to every kindle device that's linked to your Amazon account. I'm in Australia, and I've found that sometimes books that are unavailable on amazon.com become available when I check my local store, and visa versa.

How to borrow a book from amazon

You can borrow a book from the kindle store if you're a *Prime* member or a *Kindle Unlimited* subscriber (Chapter 10). Amazon automatically applies your membership and subscriptions to the kindle store buy button on a book's sales page, and will show the correct price for your membership level. Kindle unlimited subscribers can borrow any book labelled *Kindle Unlimited,* and Prime members can borrow a constantly changing subset of *Kindle Unlimited* books.

How to borrow a book on your paperwhite

Tap the button, sometimes labelled as *Read now* and sometimes labelled as *Buy for $0.00*, and the book will download. Books are labelled as *Kindle Unlimited* if they're enrolled in the scheme. You can make the store show only those books by using of the *Prime* and *Kindle Unlimited* category filters at the top of the kindle store (label (2) in Figure 4-1).

How to borrow a book from a browser

Tap the *Read for Free* button and it will be delivered to your amazon cloud and by default to all your kindle devices.

Over broadband internet, your book should download and appear on your home screen in less than a minute. Tap the thumbnail to start reading.

How to borrow a book using the amazon app

If you're a Prime member or Kindle Unlimited subscriber, you can borrow books from the Amazon app.

Once you've found a book, from the *Deliver to* tab select your paperwhite as the device you want the book to download to, and then click *Read for $0.00*. Amazon's Whispersync will deliver the book directly to your paperwhite.

You can't buy Kindle books from the amazon app. That's because app stores charge amazon a sellers fee.

How to borrow a book using the kindle app

If you're a Prime member or Kindle Unlimited subscriber, you can borrow books from the kindle app.

Once you've found a book, click *Read for $0.00*. Amazon's Whispersync will deliver the book directly to your kindle cloud – that's all your kindle devices including your paperwhite. I've found that sometimes a book won't download to my paperwhite unless I've opened it in the app first.

You can't buy Kindle books from the kindle app. That's because app stores charge amazon a sellers fee (that amazon doesn't want to pay).

How to borrow a book from your local library

Kindle books can only be borrowed from US libraries that subscribe to Overdrive. You need to be logged in to both your local library and your amazon account.

- You can send an eBook to your Kindle via Overdrive's Libby app. On the library's book page, check to see if *Kindle* is one of the supported formats. Click the link and follow the prompts.

- You can also borrow a Kindle book via Overdrive and read it on the amazon cloud reader.

For more information. . .

- Search google for the following title "Borrowing Kindle Books from your library's OverDrive website or the OverDrive app" https://help.overdrive.com/en-us/0431.html

- And Search google for this title too "libbyapp reading with kindle" https://help.libbyapp.com/en-us/6017.htm#

The 9ᵗʰ Street Books website has compiled a list of libraries that cater for non-residents. Google "library access for everyone 9th street books" to find it.

How to get free books

You don't have to be an *Amazon Prime* member or a *Kindle Unlimited* subscriber to get free Kindle books. You could simply choose to only download free books from the Amazon store! Often authors list their books for free in the hope that they will get reviews, or the book might be first in a series that they hope to get you hooked on.

Here's some places to look for free books. . .

- In the Kindle store search bar (label (2) in Figure 4-1), type terms like "free Kindle books" and "Classic literature".

- OverDrive and Libby in participating US libraries

- gutenberg.org

- standardebooks.org

- manybooks.net

- search google for "free Kindle books"

- search Facebook and other social media for "free Kindle books"

If you find a book on a non Amazon site, you're best to download it in ePub format. Then transfer it to your paperwhite using one of the techniques I described earlier in this chapter.

7.4 - How to remove a book from your paperwhite

In this section I show you how to return a Kindle Unlimited or Prime borrow, return an unwanted or accidental purchase, and how to delete or remove a book from your paperwhite. . .

How to return a book you borrowed from amazon

Home or Library > tap and hold the book thumbnail > Return to Kindle Unlimited

To return a *Kindle Unlimited* or *Prime reading* book, in your *Library* screen, tap and hold your finger on the book thumbnail to open the book menu. Then tap on *Return to kindle Unlimited*. This will remove the book from your library and end your access to it. Your notes and highlights are saved and will be reinstated if you borrow the book again.

To show only the Kindle Unlimited and Prime Reading books in your Library, tap the *filter* button (label (7) in Figure 4-1) and choose *Kindle unlimited* from the *Your Programs* area in the box.

If you need to see your Kindle Unlimited borrowing history, look in the *Content and Devices* area of your amazon account (Chapter 9).

How to return a book for a refund

Browser > Your Orders > Return for a Refund

There's three ways to return a book for a refund.

1. **If you purchased it by accident:** There's a *Purchased by accident? area* on the Thankyou Page that displays following a successful purchase. Tap the <u>*CANCEL ORDER*</u> button

to return the book and get a refund.

2. **If it is within 7 days of buying the book**: In a web browser, go to *Your Orders* in your amazon account. Then click *Return for a Refund* and from the drop-down list, choose a reason for the refund (eg. wrong item, defective, etc).

3. **If you have read more than 10% of the book:** You will need to send a customer service request. This will be reviewed by a human to ensure your return complies with Amazon's abuse policies.

How to delete a book from your library

Even though your paperwhite stores a lot of books, you might decide to free space or to tidy up.

You can choose to *remove download,* or *permanently delete* a non-kindle-unlimited book or file that you've downloaded to your paperwhite. Tap and hold on a book's thumbnail, and from the menu that appears. . .

- tap *Remove download* to keep the book in the cloud but remove it from your paperwhite.

- tap *Permanently delete* to remove it from your paperwhite and the cloud.

You can also delete a book from within any of your kindle apps, or from your amazon account in a web browser.

7.5 - Collections

Collections are a bit like folders on your desktop computer and can be a great way to organize your books. For example, you might want to create a collection called fiction and another called nonfiction.

You can create a collection from your Paperwhite or any other kindle device (eg. the kindle app on your smartphone). Once you create a collection, its available on all your kindle devices. Lets look at how to create, add and view them.

Create a collection
Home / Library > ⋮ > Create a Collection

To create a collection, from either the *Home* screen or *Library* screen, tap ⋮ in the top right corner (label (3) in Figure 4-1) and take the *Create a collection* option at the bottom of that menu. Use the keypad that appears to give your collection a name.

Add a book to a collection
Library > tap and hold a book thumbnail > Add to / Remove from collection

To add a book to a collection, in your library, tap and hold the book, and then from the popup menu, choose *add to / remove from a collection* and then tap the collection you want to add it to.

View a collection
Library > Filter > Collections

You can access the collection from your *Library* screen by selecting the *Collections* filter from the three horizontal bar menu (label (7) in Figure 4-1). Dismiss the filter box by tapping outside it. Tap on the collection thumbnail to see the books within it.

Chapter 8

The settings menu

The *Settings* menu is a collection of options and settings that you can use to customize and manage your Paperwhite. The *Settings* menu can be accessed from the. . .

- *Home* screen and *Library* screen (label (3) in Figure 4-1).

- *Quick access* toolbar within a book (label (18) in Figure 4-3).

- *Standard* toolbar (label (30) in Figure 4-4).

To simplify the remainder of this chapter, I'm going to assume that you've already found your way to each of the *Settings* sub-menus via one of those three paths.

8.1 – The *Your Account* sub-menu
: > *Settings* > *Your Account*

From the *Your Account* sub-menu, you can change your device name, connect to goodreads, add personal information, and find your Kindle email address.

Device name
: > *Settings* > *Your Account* > *Device Name*

Tap *Device name* to give your paperwhite a name. Sometimes you need to send books to an individual kindle, so make sure it's a name you'll recognize. For example, I have Kindle devices called *Ian's Paperwhite* and *Ian's desktop*.

You can also change your paperwhite's name from the *content and devices* area of your amazon account.

Personal Info

⋮ > *Settings* > *Your Account* > *Personal Info*

Tap *Personal Info* to add personal information about yourself. It's a free text box that could include your name, email address, phone number, etc.

Social networks

⋮ > *Settings* > *Your Account* > *Social Networks*

Tap *Social Networks* to connect to the 125 million strong goodreads book reviewing site.

When you're linked to goodreads, you can share that you're currently reading a book, your reading progress and your star rating for the book. Select the *Link your account* option and follow the on-screen instructions to sign in to your goodreads account.

You paperwhite's connection to goodreads is enhanced by all the extra things you can do when you're logged into the goodreads site in a web browser. In the browser version, you can connect with other readers, access interest focused lists, participate in competitions, and leave written reviews.

Deregister device

⋮ > *Settings* > *Your Account* > *Deregister Device*
OR
Amazon in a web browser > *Accounts & Lists drop-down menu* > *Man-*

age your content and devices > Devices (select device) > Deregister

To deregister your paperwhite, tap *Deregister Device.* Then tap *Deregister* to confirm that you want to deregister the device.

You deregister your paperwhite if you need to transfer its ownership to another person or account. Deregistering removes your personal information and settings, and unlinks your paperwhite from your amazon account. Afterwards, you can setup your paperwhite again and register it to a different Amazon account (see Chapter 2 and Chapter 3).

If your Kindle has been stolen, you can deregister it from the *Devices* area of your amazon account in a web browser.

Send-to-Kindle email
⋮ > *Settings > Your Account > Send-to-Kindle email*

To find your paperwhite's email address, tap *Send-to-Kindle email.*

The Send-to-Kindle email is an email address that is associated with your Kindle device or app. You can use this email address to send documents, books, and other files from your computer or other devices directly to your paperwhite without the need for a cable or other physical connection.

You can also find this address in the devices area of your amazon account in a web browser (Chapter 7). The email address that you're sending from must be in the approved send-from email list (Chapter 7).

8.2 – The *Wireless* sub-menu
⋮ > *Settings > Wireless*

The wireless sub-menu includes options for placing your paperwhite into airplane mode, connecting to a Wi-Fi network, and deleting Wi-Fi passwords.

Airplane mode
⋮ > *Settings > Wireless > Airplane Mode*

When airplane mode is toggled on, your paperwhite's Wi-Fi is turned off and it disconnects from all Wi-Fi (and cellular networks in some older models). It's essential functionality for air travel. Airplane mode can also help to conserve battery life.

Airplane mode is also available from the *Quick Actions* toolbar (label (15) in Figure 4-3).

Wi-Fi networks
⋮ > *Settings > Wireless > Wi-Fi networks*

Tap *Wi-Fi networks* to be shown a list of available Wi-Fi networks. Tap the network you want to connect to. Your paperwhite remembers networks that you've connected to before, so you'll only need to enter a password if prompted. I troubleshoot Wi-Fi connection problems in Chapter 11.

When you're connected to Wi-Fi, you're connected to the Amazon ecosystem - the kindle store, synchronized reading across kindle devices, device management, and more.

Delete Wi-Fi Passwords
⋮ > *Settings > Wireless > Delete Wi-Fi Passwords*

Tap *Delete Wi-Fi Passwords* to permanently delete ALL Wi-Fi passwords stored on your paperwhite.

8.3 – The *Device options* sub-menu
⋮ > *Settings > Device Options*

The *Device options* sub-menu lets you control your screen saver, view information about your paperwhite, set a passcode, restart it, and reset it. There's also advanced options like setting the device time, Whispersync, power saving and privacy.

Display Cover
⋮ > *Settings > Device Options > Display Cover*

Tap *Display Cover* to toggle displaying either the cover of the book you're currently reading, or a screensaver. I used to have this toggled on, but not anymore. I like to read widely and experiment with genres that I haven't read before. Recently, a book cover caught me off-guard. It was a bit too "racy" for my young daughter to see! I consider myself to be open minded, but when I looked closely, even I thought the cover was a bit challenging.

Device info
⋮ > *Settings > Device Options > Device Info*

Tap *Device Info* to view a collection of information about your paperwhite, including the model number, software version, serial number, and other details that can be useful if you need to check hardware and software versions when you're troubleshooting a problem.

Device passcode
⋮ > *Settings > Device Options > Device Passcode*

Tap *Device Passcode* to set a Personal Identification Number (PIN). Without a PIN, anyone who picks up your paperwhite can buy and review books on your amazon account, as well as reading or deleting your books and personal documents.

To set a passcode, enter a PIN, and then re-enter to confirm.

Once you have set a passcode, you will be prompted to enter it whenever you turn on the device or wake it from sleep mode.

Here's some strategies for selecting a PIN that you won't forget...

- Don't use the same PIN as you use for banking, or other things that you'd like to keep secure.

- Think of an obscure town that you visited once, or a town your grandparents lived and use its ZIP code.

In the troubleshooting chapter (Chapter 11), I show you what to do if you forget your PIN

Restart

⦂ > *Settings > Device Options > Restart*

Tap *Restart* to, well, restart your paperwhite. It's good practice to do this occasionally. It cleans up memory and can trigger it to check for updates. Sometimes restarting can also fix a flakey, slow or unresponsive device.

To restart your Paperwhite, tap *Restart* and in the box that appears tap the YES button. You can also restart your paperwhite by pressing and holding the power button, and then tapping *Restart* in the box that appears.

Reset

⦂ > *Settings > Device Options > Reset*

Tap *Reset* to restore your paperwhite to its default factory settings. WARNING, all your personal data and content will be erased. This option could be useful if you were having problems with your paperwhite and want to troubleshoot by restoring the default settings. A more likely scenario is that you want to sell your paperwhite or give it away.

Assuming that just prior to the reset, you had Wi-Fi turned on so that your paperwhite was synchronized to the cloud, when you setup your paperwhite again, all your Books, notes and highlights (except content that you copied via cable) will be restored as a part of the setup process (Chapter 3).

Advanced options

⋮ > *Settings > Device Options > Advanced Options*

Tap *Advanced Options* to set the device time, choose how book series and collections will be shown in your library, update your kindle, and toggle Whispersync on or off. There's also power saver and privacy options.

Device Time

⋮ > *Settings > Device Options > Advanced Options > Device Time*

Tap *Device Time* to set the time. Tap the up and down arrows for hours, minutes and am/pm.

Home and Library

⋮ > *Settings > Device Options > Advanced Options > Home and Library*

Tap *Home and Library* to choose how your books and collections are displayed. You can toggle to. . .

- group book series together.

- choose how you want your collections to display (3 options).

Update your kindle

⋮ > *Settings > Device Options > Advanced Options > Update Your Kindle*

Tap *Update Your Kindle* to update your paperwhite.

Occasionally, Amazon releases software updates to add new features and fix bugs. Your paperwhite should check for these automatically, so you'll only need use this button on rare occasions. If no updates are available, this option is greyed out.

To update your Paperwhite, you will need to be connected to Wi-Fi. It's bad practice to allow any device to shut down part way through an update, so make sure your paperwhite has enough charge.

Whispersync for Books
⋮ > *Settings > Device Options > Advanced Options > Whispersync for Books*

Tap *Whispersync for Books* to toggle Whispersync on and off.

Assuming that you're connected to both Wi-Fi and your Amazon account, Whispersync synchronizes your reading progress, notes, and highlights across all your kindle devices. This means that you can pick up where you left off on one device and continue reading on another, and with your latest notes and highlights available.

I troubleshoot Whispersync in Chapter 11.

Power Saver
⋮ > *Settings > Device Options > Advanced Options > Power Saver*

Tap *Power Saver* to toggle power saving functionality on and off.

- Toggle *off* to place your paperwhite into standby mode so that it turns on faster.

- Toggle *on* to place your paperwhite into low power sleep mode.

After an extensive search of forums and blogs I can honestly say that what low power mode does is a mystery. The most likely thing it would do is to turn off background Wi-Fi.

Alternative (better documented) strategies for saving power include disabling page refresh, reducing the screen brightness and placing your kindle into airplane mode.

Privacy
⋮ > Settings > Device Options > Advanced Options > Privacy

Tap *Privacy* to toggle Amazon's monitoring of your reading habits. That's the information that amazon uses to compile your reading statistics that it displays in the kindle app, and to customize its marketing to you. By customized-marketing, I mean that if you read mostly Kindle Unlimited books, Amazon will recommend more of those. Fantasy reader – Amazon will recommend more fantasy books. Have a favorite author – Amazon will show you their new book.

Tap the *Disable* button if you don't want this functionality.

8.4 – The *Reading options* sub-menu
⋮ > Settings > Reading Options

From the *Reading Options* sub-menu, you can toggle *Page Refresh* and *Vocabulary Builder* on and off.

Page refresh
⋮ > Settings > Reading Options > Page Refresh

Tap *Page Refresh* to toggle it on and off. Page refresh overcomes the ghosting problem that can occur on e-ink devices. Ghosting is where bits of the previous page you were reading still display on your screen, and make it look smudgy.

Turning *Page Refresh* off can also be a component of a power saving strategy. Personally, my priority is to have a screen that's clear, bright and easy on my eyes. Seeing as I always have access to recharging facilities (even when bush camping), I've never bothered about this power saving option. So, unless you are in a situation where its essential to conserve power, my advice is to toggle *Page refresh* on.

The *Vocabulary Builder* sub-menu
⋮ > *Settings > Reading Options > Vocabulary Builder*

Tap *Vocabulary Builder* to toggle it on and off. Vocabulary builder is a tool that records words that you've looked up in your paperwhite's dictionary. The idea is that every now and then you'll access the tool and revise the words you've looked up. I explain how to use it in Chapter 5.

I don't use this functionally often, but I do like it. I imagine that it would be very useful to students and language learners.

Vocabulary Builder is limited to 2000 words, so older words get removed once the limit is reached. The word list is not updated if you disable this feature.

8.5 – The *Languages and dictionaries* sub-menu
⋮ > *Settings > Languages and Dictionaries*

Tap the *Languages and Dictionaries* sub-menu to manage the language and dictionary settings on your paperwhite. The menus include options for changing the device's language, changing dictionaries, and changing the keyboard.

Language
⋮ > *Settings > Languages and Dictionaries > Language*

Tap *Language* to choose the language that corresponds to the book that you're reading. If you're reading a book written in English you have a choice between US English and UK English. If you're reading a book written in French, you would choose French or Canadian French, etc.

Keyboards
⋮ > *Settings > Languages and Dictionaries > Keyboards*

Tap *Keyboards* to change your paperwhite's keyboard to any one of 27 different language preferences.

Dictionaries
⋮ > *Settings > Languages and Dictionaries > Dictionaries*

Tap *Dictionaries* to choose the dictionary you want to use. In the English language, you have the choice between the Oxford Dictionary of English and the New Oxford American Dictionary. Not every one of the 50+ other dictionaries is available on your paperwhite by default. You install additional dictionaries from your web browser (Chapter 9).

Chinese Sort Order
⋮ > *Settings > Languages and Dictionaries > Chinese Sort Order*

Tap *Chinese Sort Order* to change the way that Chinese characters are displayed. You can toggle between Hanyu Pinyin, Stroke order and Zhuyin Fuhao.

8.6 – The *Accessibility* sub-menu
⋮ > *Settings > Accessibility*

Tap the *Accessibility* sub-menu to configure your Paperwhite's text-to-speech tool, or to invert your screen's color.

VoiceView text-to-speech Screen Reader
⠿ > *Settings > Accessibility > VoiceView Screen Reader*

Tap *VoiceView Screen Reader* to have menu items and books read to you.

To enable VoiceView you need to first pair your Kindle to a Bluetooth audio device (headphones, speaker, etc). This can be tricky in the absence of being shown the exact process. I used my intuition and toggled the reader on, and tried to connect from the box that launched there. I WAS WRONG!!! I eventually got it to work, but I found the process frustrating, fickle and clunky. I was testing with late model Bose headphones and no-name ear plugs. However, I used a gen 10 paperwhite for the first draft of this book, and recently took delivery of a gen 11 paperwhite. *VoiceView* did work better on the gen 11 – I suspect that was probably due to its faster processor.

Here's how to pair your blue tooth audio device...

1. Set your audio device into pairing mode.

2. Toggle *VoiceView Screen Reader* on and a message box will appear saying that your Bluetooth audio device has been recognized.

3. Tap two fingers on the screen for 1 second (index and middle finger worked best for me).

4. Wait and follow any further instructions.

5. After initial pairing, your device does not need to go through subsequent pairings.

Toggle the VoiceView Screen Reader button on to hear kindle text being read to you. When you toggle the button to be on, the tutorial, speech rate, volume and Bluetooth devices menus are enabled. The voice is a bit wooden, a problem that I imagine will be fixed as the current generation of AI voices matures.

Now when you touch a menu item, your kindle will read it to you. First it reads the name of the menu, and then it asks you to tap twice to select the item. I found that I needed to wait until the "tap twice" instruction finished before successfully double-tapping the menu item. When you're in a book VoiceView will also read it to you.

There are videos that demonstrate this on YouTube. Search for "voiceview screen reader kindle paperwhite". For example the @readerzplanet video at

You can probably tell that I'm not a fan of VoiceView. You might find it more useful to explore text-to-speech in the kindle app on your smart device. You'll need to enable the text-to-speech functionality in your smart device's accessibility menu.

Tutorial
⋮ > *Settings* > *Accessibility* > *VoiceView Screen Reader* > *Tutorial*

Tap *Tutorial* to access the four *VoiceView* tutorials ...

1. Basic gestures

2. Text entry with VoiceView

3. Advanced gestures

4. General kindle information.

Speech rate

⋮ > *Settings > Accessibility > VoiceView Screen Reader > Speech Rate*

Tap *Speech Rate* to choose one of the ten speech rates on the VoiceView screen reader. There are two slower speeds, one normal speed, and seven faster speeds.

Volume
⋮ > *Settings > Accessibility > VoiceView Screen Reader > Volume*

Tap *Volume* to adjust the volume on the VoiceView screen reader. Toggle to one of the eight volume levels. On my Bluetooth headphones, the volume control did not override this, and the up and down volume buttons toggled muting on and off instead.

Bluetooth Devices
⋮ > *Settings > Accessibility > VoiceView Screen Reader > Bluetooth Devices*

Tap *Bluetooth Devices* to change to another Bluetooth audio device that's already been paired.

Invert Black and White

⋮ > *Settings > Accessibility > Invert Black and White*

Tap *Invert Black and White* to toggle between white screen with black writing and black screen with white writing. You can also do this from the *Quick Actions* toolbar (label (16) in Figure 4-3).

8.7 – The *Parental Controls* sub-menu
⋮ > *Settings > Parental Controls*

The *Parental Controls* sub-menu lets you to supervise your child's access to books and functionality on your paperwhite. Amazon kids, where it's available, lets you manually add and remove books or automatically give your child access to age-appropriate content in the store. The *restrictions* area acts as a general security item at the device level.

Amazon Kids
⋮ > *Settings > Parental Controls > Amazon Kids*

Unfortunately, amazon kids is only available in some countries (not where I live). Where it is available it appears as a separate *Amazon Kids* item in the *Parental Controls* area. From there you can add a child's name and date of birth. This lets you automatically restrict some content according to age appropriateness. Alternatively, you may choose to give them access to individual books.

You can also manage your child's content from the digital content area of your amazon account (in a browser). From the *more actions* menu next to a book, take the *Manage family library* option and add the book to an *Amazon Kid's Library.*

This appears to be a well-thought-out feature. I'm disappointed that I can't give you a better overview. Following are links to two YouTube channels. A search for *Parental controls* in each channel will produce a half dozen or so useful short videos

- **@HardResetinfo:** https://www.youtube.com/@HardresetInfo

- **goodereader:** https://www.youtube.com/goodereader

Restrictions
⋮ > *Settings > Parental Controls > Restrictions*

Tap *Restrictions* to limit the functionality of your paperwhite.

In those countries where Amazon Kids is not available, you can set controls at the device level. That's great, not just for kids, but also for when you lend your paperwhite to another adult, but say, are happy for them to access all the paperwhite's functionality, except the ability to buy a book. You can toggle the options on and off, but you'll need to enter your parental control PIN to do that. Here's what the options do. . .

- **Web browser:** Removes access to the web browser from the : menu, and from any links within a book.

- **Store:** Removes access to the store so that books cannot be bought or borrowed

- **Cloud:** Users will not be able to access their content in the cloud, and will only be able to access content that is stored on the device itself.

- **Goodreads:** Removes access to the goodreads site. You cannot add *currently reading* status or review a book.

Change PIN
: > *Settings > Parental Controls > Change PIN*

Tap *Change PIN* and you will be prompted to enter your current PIN. After you have entered your current PIN, you will be able to enter a new PIN of your choice.

Enter the new PIN and then again in the confirmation box and your PIN will be changed.

Chapter 9

Managing your experience from a web browser

You can manage your Paperwhite, access your reading history, and review your notes and highlights when you're logged into your local Amazon store in a web browser. Some tasks *require* the use of a browser, while others *are better suited to* the browser based kindle cloud reader.

This chapter is about the amazon site on a desktop web browser. If you are using a browser on a smart device, depending on the device, expect that some functionality may be missing.

9.1 - Manage your paperwhite from your amazon account

In the *manage content and devices* area of your local store, amongst many other things, you can install additional language dictionaries, deregister your paperwhite so you can sell it, and view the books on your paperwhite, including your entire Kindle Unlimited and Prime reading borrowing history.

Install a different language dictionary

Amazon in a web browser > Accounts & Lists drop-down menu > Manage content and devices > Content > Dictionaries and User Guides

From the *Manage content and devices* area of your amazon account, click *Content, then Dictionaries and User Guides* to view the 50+ available dictionaries. Select a dictionary and then choose to *Deliver to Device*.

Manage all your kindle devices
Amazon in a web browser > Accounts and Lists > Manage content and devices > Devices

You can manage your kindle devices and apps (oasis, desktop, smartphone, etc.) from the devices area of your local amazon account. In a browser, login to your account, and from the *Accounts and Lists* dropdown menu, click *Manage content and devices* and then *Devices*. Click the large *Kindle* button and you'll see your paperwhite listed.

Choose your paperwhite and you can view its model and serial number, change its label (eg. "Ian's Paperwhite" to "Ian's gen 11 Paperwhite"), deregister it (if you sell it, or it was stolen), set it as the default device that all content will be automatically delivered to, and view all the content on it (books, documents and dictionaries).

Kindle orders placed by me
Amazon in a web browser > Accounts and lists > Manage content and devices > Content

In a browser, login to your amazon account, and from the *Accounts and Lists* dropdown menu, click *Manage content and devices,* and then *Content.*

Here you'll find a list of all the books you've ever bought, and active Kindle Unlimited and Prime reading loans. It's where you manage your books – return a loan, deliver a book to or remove a book from any of your kindle devices, add or remove a book from a collection, clear the furthest page read, mark a book as read, and view the details of a book order. Aside from viewing the details of a book order, this functionality is identical to that on your paperwhite.

If you're a Kindle Unlimited subscriber or Prime member, by default, you're shown your current borrowings. You can also view books that you've returned. To do this, choose to view *Kindle Unlimited [or Prime Reading]* from the drop-down menu just above your books, and then *Returned* from the drop-down menu to its right.

How to cancel kindle unlimited membership
Amazon in a web browser > Accounts & Lists drop-down menu > Subscriptions > Your membership and Subscriptions > Kindle Unlimited > Kindle Unlimited Settings > Cancel > Kindle Unlimited Membership

In your browser, login to your local amazon account, and from the *Accounts and Lists* dropdown menu, click *Subscriptions,* then *Your membership and Subscriptions*, then *Kindle Unlimited,* then *Kindle Unlimited Settings,* then *Cancel,* and then *Kindle Unlimited Membership.*

When you cancel your subscription, books that you've borrowed will be removed from your paperwhite the next time it connects to Wi-Fi. So, if there's a Kindle Unlimited book that you really want to finish, you should place your paperwhite into airplane mode (label (15) in Figure 4-3) before you cancel your subscription.

Amazon realizes that people hop in and out of subscription services, so if you resubscribe in the future your Kindle Unlimited borrows, and notes and highlights will be reinstated.

9.2 - The Kindle cloud reader

Logged into amazon . . .   https://read.amazon.com/

The kindle cloud reader lets you read any kindle book in your library (except documents that you've uploaded) in a web browser. Sign into your Amazon account and go to read.amazon.com.

The main reason that I've included the kindle cloud reader in this book, is that it has much better note taking and highlighting functionality than your paperwhite. Not only do you have better control over what you're highlighting. You can correct, expand on and color-code your notes. For me, using a keyboard and mouse to correct and elaborate on notes is much easier than using my stumpy fingers to take detailed notes on my paperwhite.

The sidebar and top bar of the Kindle Cloud Reader change depending on whether you're in your library or reading a book.

Kindle cloud reader - library mode

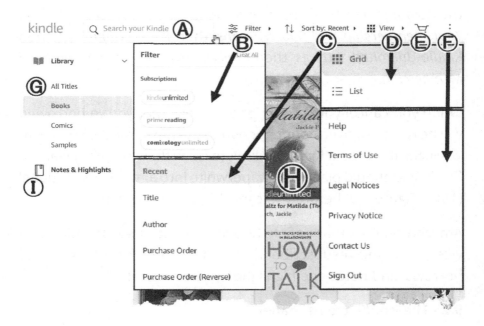

Figure 9-1: The Kindle cloud reader - library mode.
The labels are described below. You can download this figure from ianallanauthor.com/paperwhite.

While you're in Library mode, the top menu bar contains options for filtering your books by subscription type, sorting, grid view and list view, and kindle store. The sidebar has options to display either books or notes. The main area displays all the kindle books in your library that you've purchased, or currently have on loan from Prime Reading, Kindle Unlimited or ComiXology Unlimited.

The menus and options available in the Kindle Cloud Reader include:

Label (A) Search box: Type the name of any book in your library into the search box to find it.

Label (B) Filter: Filter books according to your subscription.

Label (C) Sort: Sort your books in various ways – recent, title, author, or order of purchase.

Label (D) Display: Toggle to display as either a grid or a list.

Label (E) Kindle store: Click the shopping trolley to be taken to the Kindle store. Books are delivered to your cloud reader, but you can also choose to have them delivered to any of your kindle devices and apps from the drop-down menu on the thankyou page.

Label (F) Help, notices, and sign out: This menu provides access to resources and support for the Kindle Cloud Reader, including a user guide, FAQs, and contact information for customer service.

Label (G) Side bar: In the side bar you can elect to show all titles or filter kindle books, ComiXology books and samples.

Label (H) The main area: This is where all the books in your library are displayed.

Label (I) Notes and highlights: Here's where you view the notes and highlights that you made in books that you've read, including kindle unlimited and prime reading books that you've returned. Clicking on a book launches the box shown in Figure 9-2.

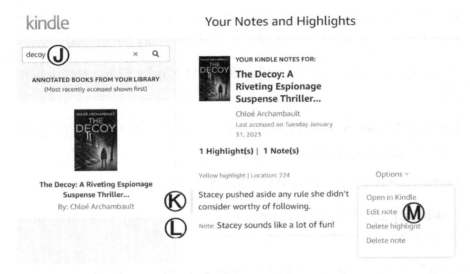

Figure 9-2: Notes and highlights in a browser.

The labels are described below. You can download this figure from ianallanauthor.com/paperwhite.

When you're in *Notes and Highlights* mode, a list of all the titles you've added notes and highlights to, appears in the sidebar. When you tap on a thumbnail, your notes and highlights for the book appear in the body of the screen.

I have to say that only now, as I'm writing this, do I realize what amazing functionality this is. It hadn't occurred to me that my notes and highlights would build up over time. I can't resist giving you a few examples. . .

> "Leave pettiness to the petty". Jay Christoph. *Nevernight*.

> "Men could be wonderful fathers. Sarah just hadn't picked the right one." Melinda Leigh, *She can kill*.

> "I'd like to say that Natalie isn't pretty. But that would be a lie . . . It's only when she opens her mouth that she turns ugly." Suzanne Redfern, *In an Instant*

> And, on the topic of the protagonist's very bad driving. . . "My driving instructor, a bald man with severe halitosis and nerves of steel labelled the impediment 'Pedal dyslexia' ". Suzanne Redfern, *In an Instant*.

I am having such a blast catching up on the essence of my years of Kindle reading. There are so many one-liners that I had forgotten. But, best I get back to writing his book. Let's talk about the labels in Figure 9-2.

Label (J) Search: You can type the name of a book to search for in your library. Even Kindle Unlimited and Prime reading books that you've returned.

Label (K) Highlight words and phrases in a book: *Stacey pushed aside any rule she didn't consider worthy of following* is a sentence that I highlighted.

Label (L) Comment on a highlighted word or phrase: *Stacey sounds like a lot of fun* is a comment I made about the text that

I highlighted.

Label (M) Note options: From the *options* menu you can choose to open the book in kindle, edit the note, delete the highlight or delete the note.

Kindle cloud reader – book mode

The Kindle Cloud Reader offers many of the same features as the Kindle app, including the ability to adjust font size, background color, note taking, book marking and dictionaries. Click on a book's thumbnail to open it. The book mode menu is labelled in Figure 9-3.

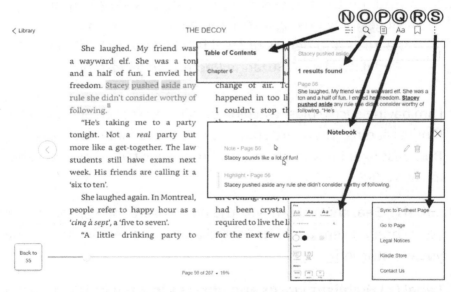

Figure 9-3: Expanded versions of menus in the Kindle Cloud reader.

The labels are described below. You can download this figure from ianallanauthor.com/paperwhite.

Label (N) Table of contents.

Label (O) Search: Search for a word or phrase within a book.

Label (P) Notebook - Highlight and annotate: Highlight and annotate text and edit your annotations. You can also choose to color code your note yellow, blue, pink or orange.

Label (Q) Font: Change the font, its size, page color and layout of the page.

Label (R) Bookmark: Add or remove a bookmark.

Label (S) Additional menu: Sync to the cloud, go to a page, legal notices, kindle store and contact amazon.

Could you spare a moment to review my book?

Don't forget the resources page at ianallanauthor.com/paperwhite

I would be so grateful if you would leave a review on Amazon. . .

Chapter 10

Subscriptions and Categories of Books in the Store

Amazon in a web browser > Kindle Store > Kindle books

Before you get used to buying all your books directly from your paperwhite, you should know about Amazon's book subscriptions and major book categories. Understanding these has expanded my reading horizons - I read more widely and more often than I ever did. Who knows what might happen for you?

Amazon's subscriptions include Kindle Unlimited and Prime. Major categories include Kindle Short Reads, Kindle Vella, Kindle First Reads, Kindle Singles, Amazon Charts and eBooks that come bundled with audible. You access these from a browser. Unfortunately, not all subscriptions and categories are available in every country.

10.1 - Subscriptions

Out of Kindle Unlimited and Prime subscriptions, you may find that Prime is a good place to start. It's a bit cheaper than Kindle Unlimited, has wide ranging benefits, and includes a subset of Kindle Unlimited, Graphic Novels and Audio – enough to give you an understanding of how those subscriptions work. Once you're subscribed, the kindle store on your paperwhite and other devices automatically recognizes your subscription, and the buy button on eligible books changes to *read now for $0.00.*

Kindle unlimited

Kindle Unlimited is a subscription library service offered by Amazon that gives you access to eBooks, audiobooks, and magazines. There's around four million titles that are labeled as *Kindle Unlimited* in the kindle store. Eligible books are clearly labelled with *Kindle Unlimited* above their thumbnail.

When a kindle unlimited subscriber is logged in to their account, for eligible books, the text in the *Buy* button automatically changes to *Read Now for $0*, or to *$0.00 Kindle Unlimited*. Undoubtedly there'll be different versions of the button over time.

When you find an eligible book you want to read, tap on the book thumbnail to open its sales page and then tap the *Read now* button to download the book and start reading. You could also choose to buy the book if its one that you want to keep beyond your Kindle Unlimited membership.

You can borrow 20 books at a time for a flat monthly fee – currently ~$10 US / month. Beyond 20 books, you'll be prompted to return one so you can borrow another. There is no such thing as a kindle yearly subscription. The monthly fee is debited automatically using the payment method nominated on your account.

From the Amazon store in your paperwhite (label (2) in Figure 4-1), browser, or app, you can filter to show you only Kindle Unlimited eligible books.

You subscribe to *kindle unlimited* by logging into your Amazon account and then clicking on *Kindle Unlimited* in the side menu, or type *Kindle Unlimited* into the Amazon store's search bar and follow the prompts.

Prime Reading

Prime members have access to a subset of the Kindle Unlimited library, and one free First Reads book a month. There are 3000 or so regularly rotated titles to choose from, some of which come bundled with audio. Prime is a good way to get a taste for the Kindle Unlimited experience, especially seeing as many people are already members for its delivery, movie, music and other benefits.

If you're a Prime member, in all the apps and stores there's a *Prime Reading* filter that you can tap to see only *Prime* results.

Amazon Prime Reading replaced the Kindle Owners Lending Library (KOLL) in 2020.

Kindle newsstand

Kindle Newstand was closed in mid-2023.

10.2 - Featured categories

The featured categories in the kindle department in the browser version of the amazon store contain some novel ways of searching for your next read.

Books with narration
Amazon in a web browser > Kindle Store > eBooks with Audible

In your browser, login to your local amazon account, and from the dropdown menu attached to the search bar click *Kindle Store* and press enter, and then *eBooks with Audible* from the top menu. There's also a *books with audible narration* category in the kindle app.

Audible is not enabled on the Paperwhite in my marketplace, but it is linked within the Kindle app on my smart phone. Kindle books with narration have a headphone symbol next to the title and there's an "add audible narration" upgrade tick on the sales page. There are around 2600 titles (March 2023) where the Audible version is included for free to Kindle Unlimited subscribers. A small subset of these is available to Prime members.

In the kindle app on your smart device, tap the top of the screen for the standard toolbar. An *Audible Narration – tap download link* appears at the bottom of the screen. When you play the audio, the app highlights each word as it is being read. What a great tool for language learners!

You can use Amazon matchmaker to interrogate all the books in your library and match them with an audible narration if one is available. Audio books discovered by Matchmaker are often a fraction of the stand alone audible price. You need to be logged in to your amazon account and on a browser. I could give you the long and complicated web link, but you're better to just google *"amazon matchmaker"* to find it.

Kindle Short Reads
Amazon in a web browser > Kindle Store > Kindle Short Reads

In your browser, login to your local amazon account, and from the dropdown menu next to the search bar click *Kindle Store* and press enter. Then click on *Kindle Short Reads* in the side menu. Otherwise, type *short reads* into the search bar and it should appear at the top of the search results.

Short reads are kindle books categorized on amazon's website by page length and estimated read time – 15, 30, 45, 60, 90, and 120 minutes.

Sometimes this category can be hard to find. If all else fails, google *Kindle Short Reads*.

Amazon First Reads

Amazon in a web browser > Kindle Store > Kindle Books > Amazon First Reads

In your browser, login to your local amazon account, and from the dropdown menu attached to the search bar click *Kindle Store* and press enter, then *Kindle Books,* and then the *Amazon First Reads* link in the top menu bar. Otherwise, type *first reads* into the search bar and it should appear at the top of the search results.

First reads allows you to download, read and keep one new pre-release book every month. It provides access to a selection of new books that have not yet been released to the general public. Each book, written by well-known authors, is $2 from the amazon storefront, or free for Prime members from either the storefront or the app. You have to be a first reads member to gain access. Joining is free, but by joining, you're giving amazon permission to send you a monthly email about the program. There's two ways to participate. . .

- **Prime members:** Prime members get one first-read per month for free.

- **Non-members:** Join Amazon first reads from the first reads area of the kindle store. You need to be logged in to your local Amazon store to do this. Once you're joined, you can buy one first release book per month for $2.

Kindle singles

Amazon in a web browser > Kindle Store > Kindle Books > Kindle Singles

In your browser, login to your local amazon account, and from the dropdown menu attached to the search bar click *Kindle Store* and press enter, then *Kindle Books,* and then, in the side bar *Kindle Singles*.

Kindle Singles are novellas and essays that are usually shorter than traditional books, but longer than magazine articles. They are often written by well-known authors, journalists, or experts in their field.

The category can be hard to find. It's a link at the very bottom of the *Kindle Store* on your paperwhite.

Kindle Vella (serials)
Amazon in a web browser > Kindle Store > Kindle Books > Kindle Vella

In your browser, login to your local amazon account, and from the dropdown menu attached to the search bar click *Kindle Store* and press enter, then *Kindle Books,* and then, in the top bar *Kindle Vella*. If all else fails, google *Kindle Vella*.

Kindle Vella is serialized fiction. You can follow stories in bite-sized installments, with new chapters being released on a regular schedule.

The first few episodes of every story are free. You unlock later episodes with "Tokens" that can only be used in Vella. See more at www.amazon.com/kindle-vella.

Unfortunately, Kindle Vella is only available in the US for people with a US account.

Chapter 11

Troubleshooting

If you're here for a reason other than curiosity, its likely that you're anxious, frustrated and possibly a little angry. Take it from someone who, in a former life, was responsible for supporting the foreign exchange area of a major bank, maintaining calm in your crisis is your friend. Be methodical and document your steps, and you're far more likely to solve your problem. So, take a deep breath and read on. . .

11.1 - Setup problems

I accidently setup in a foreign language

If you accidently chose a foreign language during setup, and you can't read the menus to understand where reset is, here's the menu path...

Home / Library > : > Settings (5th item down) > Device Options (3rd item down) > Reset (2nd last item) > then tap YES (bottom right item in the box)

PIN problems

You cannot reset your PIN if you've forgotten it. You'll need to reset your paperwhite.

- Enter 111222777 into the passcode area to erase your paperwhite and restore the factory settings.

- Once reset, follow the prompts to get connected again (Chapter 3), and your kindle will re-populate from the cloud, but without a PIN. This may take a while if you have lots of books to download.

11.2 - Content problems

Strange symbols in my book

There are two possible reasons for strange symbols in your book.
. .

- **Wrong language setting:** The language of your paperwhite may not be set to the language the book was written in. Change your paperwhite's language in the *Languages and Dictionaries* area of the *Settings* menu (Chapter 8).

- **Author error:** The author may have written the book in an incompatible word processor. For example, kindle does not recognize some of the smart formatting (eg smart quotes) in MS word, and displays them as strange symbols.

What happens to my books if get a new paperwhite or I lose my old one?

Browser: *Amazon > Your account > Manage your content and devices > Devices*
Paperwhite: *Swipe down for the Quick Actions toolbar > Sync (label (17) in Figure 4-3)*

All your kindle purchases are attached to your amazon account in the cloud, and so, aside from content that you've transferred to you paperwhite via cable, none of your books will be lost. When you connect your paperwhite to your amazon account during setup, all your content is downloaded and synchronized with all your kindle devices. That includes notes, bookmarks, and even the page you last read. Initially only thumbnails are downloaded, so you may need to tap on a book's thumbnail to download the entire book.

If your books don't automatically appear, try the following things.
. .

- **In a browser, set your paperwhite as the default device:** From your local amazon web page, click *Your account,* then *Manage your content and devices,* then in the *Amazon Devices* tab, click on your paperwhite. In the *settings* area of the screen that launches, click the *Set as default device* button.

- **In a browser, manually deliver one or all of your books to your paperwhite:** From your local amazon web page, click *Your account,* then *Manage your content and devices*, then from the *Content* tab, select one or all of your books. Then click the *Deliver to Device* button and choose your paperwhite from the list (Chapter 7).

- **On your paperwhite:** Swipe down from the top of any screen to access the *quick actions* toolbar. Tap the synchronize icon (label (17) *in Figure 4-3*) to manually synchronize your paperwhite with all your kindle apps and devices.

Exceptions are books that you have transferred to your kindle via USB cable. That's because cable-transfers are not backed up in the cloud.

Why won't my book transfer via cable?

There is a disconnect between the many *"use a USB cable to get a book on your paperwhite"* style blog posts, and reality. It's not as simple as some bloggers make it out to be. Or maybe they just have a well-oiled workflow that works for them? There are two reasons why cable transfer often does not work, and sometimes it can be hard to tell which of the two it is.

- **You might have a corrupt eBook file:** E-book formatting is a temperamental and fickle art. Even people who create eBooks all the time dread the kindle compatibility testing stage. That's because every book creation software creates eBooks slightly differently. Something as simple as one incompatible character can cause an eBook to fail. If your paperwhite doesn't recognize the file that you're transferring, try importing it into the free Calibre software (google *Calibre*), then export the file as an ePub and transfer that.

- **File location:** Different bloggers suggest copying your book to different locations on your paperwhite. The *documents* folder, and a folder inside the *documents* folder with the same name as your file are two common recommendations. For me, some of those locations worked for some files, and not for others.

I recommend that you do not use the cable transfer technique, and instead use the *send to kindle* drag-and-drop or email techniques (Chapter 7).

Why won't the book I bought show up on my paperwhite?

Amazon in a web browser > Accounts & Lists drop-down menu > Manage your content and devices > Books > Deliver or Remove from device

Sometimes Amazon delivers your book to the wrong device. You may need to manually deliver it to your paperwhite. From your local amazon web page, click *Your account,* then *Manage your content and devices*, then from the *Content* tab, select one or all of your books and then click the *Deliver to Device* button and choose your paperwhite from the list.

Why won't the file I'm emailing appear on my paperwhite?

If you've emailed a file and it's not appearing on your paperwhite, check for the following problems. . .

- **Unauthorized email address:** Are you sending from an authorized email address? Your kindle will only accept emails from an authorized address. So, if you haven't already, you'll need to go to your amazon account and add the email address you're sending from (Chapter 7).

- **Wrong kindle email:** Are you sending to the correct kindle address? Kindle email addresses often contain the number zero and the letter O. You may be typing O's instead of zeros or visa versa? The letter O is fat and the number 0 is skinny.

- **Wi-Fi:** Do you have Wi-Fi signal?

- **Wrong file type:** Are you sending a file type that your paperwhite can read?

- **Corrupt file:** The file you're sending might be corrupt. Try importing it into the free Calibre software (google *Calibre*), then exporting it as an ePub file. Now email the ePub that you just exported.

Why won't my book synchronize to all my devices?

Sometimes Whispersync needs to be given a manual nudge to get all your devices synchronized. For example, you may have borrowed a book on one device, returned it on a different device while it was open on a different device again, and then borrowed it again (yes, that can happen). From any place on your paperwhite, swipe down for the *Quick Actions* toolbar and then tap *Sync* (label (17) in Figure 4-3).

11.3 - Charging problems

If there's no green light or amber light near the charge point, it means that your paperwhite is not charging. Here's some things to check. . .

- **Are all the connections clean:** Dust and grit can get into the charge points on both your charger and your paperwhite. Dust the socket connection on your paperwhite with an artist's brush or do a hard (spit-free) mouth-blow into it. Clean the pin connection on the cable with a soft cloth.

- **Is the cable inserted properly:** Make sure it's not loose.

- **Faulty cable:** Try a different one.

- **Faulty charger:** Try a different one.

- **Gen 11 paperwhite charger:** Even though USB-C is an adaptive power protocol, it's wise to avoid no-name chargers, and chargers > 9w (especially ones labelled *fast charger* or similar). If you do use a higher power USB-C charger, be sure to supervise it closely the first few times you use it.

- **Gen 10 paperwhite charger:** Any non USB-C charger

should not exceed 9w. Your paperwhite may go into protection mode if it does.

- **Computer USB port:** Make sure that you're not using a low power USB port. Swap to a different port.

11.4 - Hardware problems

Why does my battery drain so quickly?

Amazon's battery life claims are based on a half hour of daily reading, and your paperwhite being in airplane mode, and with the light setting at level 13. I read for 2+ hours most days, airplane mode is never enabled, and my screen brightness is set at 20 – I charge my gen 10 paperwhite most weeks. My partner reads for 2+ hours a few days a week, airplane mode is never enabled, her screen brightness is set at 18, and she often uses a large font (and so has more page turns). She charges her gen 11 paperwhite once a month.

If your battery life cannot be explained by the way you use your paperwhite, then check these things. . .

- **Cover faulty:** If you're using a cover, is it somehow inter-fering with sleep mode and causing your paperwhite to turn on and off all the time?

- **Cover for wrong paperwhite model:** Are you using a cov-er that's designed for your paperwhite model? When you're buying a cover, be sure to check that its specifications match your kindle model. A mismatch might cause sleep mode to malfunction and drain your battery.

- **Storing on the power button:** Are you storing your paper-white on its end (eg. in your bag) so that the power button is flicking on and off?

- **Brightness too high:** Lower your screen brightness (Chapter 4).

- **Wi-Fi issue:** You could have a "confused" Wi-Fi connection that's causing excessive communication between your paperwhite and your router. Reset your Wi-Fi by turning the router off. Remove the plug from the power outlet for a minute or so, so that it completely drains of power, and then reconnect it. Then check that your paperwhite is properly connected to your router (see the Why can't I get my Wi-Fi to work heading below).

- **Confused operating system:** All devices perform better if they're restarted occasionally. So, restart your paperwhite (Chapter 3).

- **Overcharged battery:** You might have overcharged your paperwhite. This is less likely, but not impossible with USB-C in the gen 11 paperwhite.

As with any battery device, consistently overcharging your paperwhite (ie. leaving it charging long after it reaches 100%), will shorten its battery life. Some commentators suggest that its good practice to run the battery completely down once every month or so.

I notice that battery replacement kits are advertised for gen 10 and older paperwhites, but not yet for gen 11 models.

Why don't my screen taps work?

Sometimes you can tap multiple times thinking that your tap has not registered, and then your paperwhite flicks through multiple pages. Most likely that's because your paperwhite is busy with the cloud while you're tapping. I've noticed that this happens less often on the gen 11 paperwhite than on the gen 10. Other times, it simply won't respond to your taps and swipes. Here's some things to think about. . .

- **It might be because your fingertip is dry or calloused:** Paperwhites use capacitive touch screen technology. That means that your finger completes an electrical circuit when you touch the screen. So, a dry or calloused finger will act as an insulator rather than as a conductor. Here's some simple things to try. . .

  - **Use a different part of your finger**: Try the side of your finger instead of the tip.

  - **Use a different finger**: Some fingers might be better conductors than others.

  - **Use a lighter touch**: You might be pressing too hard.

  - **Use a Pen Stylus:** There are pens that mimic a finger-tap on touch screen devices. My stylus works on my iPhone and my Kindle. Search online for "pen stylus". Mine cost around $15, but they can be as low as $5.

- **Is your screen dirty?** Clean a dirty screen with a soft tissue or moist cloth.

- **Is your battery low?** A low battery can cause problems on any device. Or, Maybe your outlet, cable or charger is faulty and so you think your paperwhite is charged when it is not. Does the orange charging light appear when its plugged in? One piece of hardware at a time (power outlet, cable, charger), try swapping them out.

- **Is the charge port dirty?** Clean it. Often a strong blow from your mouth is enough to dislodge dust and dirt.

- **Is your Paperwhite hot?** Most devices go into protection mode if they're left in the hot sun. Rest your paperwhite somewhere where it can cool down and try again later.

- **Is your screen bright enough for you to see the text?** Adjust it to be brighter (label (26) in Figure 4-4).

- **If all those suggestions fail:** Restart or reset your paper-white (Chapter 3)

- **Get a new paperwhite:** If none of these suggestions work, then you may need to replace your paperwhite. . .

  - **Within warranty:** Contact amazon support. Document the troubleshooting steps you've taken. Hopefully they will replace it.

  - **Damaged outside warranty conditions:** If something happened like your paperwhite was dropped or sat on, emersed in salt water too long, or the USB port is phys-ically damaged, you may need to buy a new one.

Why can't I get my Wi-Fi to work?
: > *Settings > Wireless > Wi-Fi networks*

I know. It would be easy to have a meltdown when you're trou-bleshooting a Wi-Fi connection. But it's important to be calm and methodical. Look for the most obvious problems first. Here's some things to check. . .

- **Are you in Wi-Fi range?** Make sure your paperwhite is within range of a Wi-Fi network, that there's strong signal, and that the network is functioning properly (it has power and is connected to the internet). You can check this by using the web on another device that you know is connected to the same network you're trying to connect to. Place your paperwhite next to the other device while you test both. If the other device is working, then go to the next step.

- **Are you connected to the correct Wi-Fi?** Make sure your Paperwhite is connected to the correct Wi-Fi network – the one you just tested. Select *Settings* from within the ⋮ menu (label (3) in Figure 4-1), tap *Wireless and then tap Wi-Fi Networks.* Tap on the correct network if you need to.

- **Wi-Fi won't accept your password:** If the network won't accept your password . . .

  ◦ Are you trying to connect to the correct network?

  ◦ Are you typing the password correctly? Passwords are often case sensitive. And, have you accidently confused the capital letter O and the number zero? The number 0 is skinny and the letter O is fat. Take a photo of the password with your smartphone. That way you'll be able to zoom in to see the small text.

- **You can't find the Wi-Fi password:** Look on your refrigerator (front and sides). Network providers often include a fridge magnet with your Wi-Fi name and password printed on it. Otherwise, look for a sticker on the side of the Wi-Fi router. Take a photo of it with your smartphone. That way you'll be able to zoom in to see the small text.

- **Restart your Wi-Fi:** Restart your Wi-Fi router by unplugging it from the power source for a minute or so, and then plugging it back in. Be sure to remove the plug from the power outlet completely. For some routers, just using the on/off switch is not enough. Removing the plug from the power outlet and waiting for the power to drain from the device can force it to do a full reset and check for firmware updates.

- **Reset your Wi-Fi:** Unfold a paperclip or something similar and poke it into the tiny hole on your router labelled "reset". Google "how to reset *[your router make and model]*" for exact instructions.

- **Your router frequency could be incompatible:** Check what frequency your Wi-Fi router is operating in. 11th generation Paperwhites operate in both the 2.4 Ghz and 5 Ghz frequencies. Earlier models only operate in the 2.4 Ghz frequency.

- **You might be too far away from your router:** The 5ghz frequency is fast and works well over short distances. In my home, the router is downstairs and we have problems receiving the 5ghz frequency upstairs on the opposite end of the house. We have no problems with the 2.4ghz frequency - its slower, but it copes better with thick walls, and longer distances.

- **Try a smartphone hotspot:** Create a Wi-Fi hotspot with your smartphone and test if you can connect to that.

  - **iPhone:** settings > personal hotspot
  - **Android:** settings > network and internet > hotspot &

tethering > Wi-Fi hotspot

- **You may be trying to connect to the wrong frequency:** Newer Wi-Fi routers operate in the 2.4Ghz and 5/6Ghz frequencies simultaneously. For pre-11th generation Paperwhites, check that you're trying to connect to the 2.4Ghz frequency.

- **Your router is old:** Some older Wi-Fi routers do not support the 2.4Ghz frequency. Google the make and model of your router to find this out. Replace your router if you need to.

- **Your router is in a hidden network:** Some networks operate in *hidden mode*. Add these wireless networks manually if a *rescan* does not detect them. To find your router's IP address, google *how to find my router IP address on [smartphone | windows | iOS | android]*.

If all of these suggestions have failed and your Wi-Fi will not connect to your paperwhite, or any other device, contact your internet service provider for assistance. Otherwise, you may need to try a forum such as . It will help people to help you if you have documented the steps you've taken, and EXACTLY how you went about them (including in what order).

Chapter 12

Frequently Asked Questions

Here's some answers to common questions about the paperwhite. I found them by researching forums, amazon product pages, and amazon help pages.

12.1 - Content

Does a paperwhite need Wi-Fi to work?

Your paperwhite does not need Wi-Fi if the book you're reading is already on your device. However, you cannot download kindle books to your paperwhite if you don't have Wi-Fi. Most kindle books are protected by Digital Rights Management (DRM). That means that you can only read kindle books that have been pur-chased from the kindle store using your amazon account. But, without Wi-Fi you can connect your computer to your paperwhite via cable, and then transfer eBooks and documents that you've sourced from non-amazon sites (Chapter 7).

How do I get books onto my paperwhite?

- **Buy a book from the kindle store:** Do this from on your paperwhite or from the amazon store in a browser (Chap-ter 4 and Chapter 7)

- **Borrow a Prime reading or Kindle Unlimited book:** If

you're a Prime member or a Kindle Unlimited subscriber, you can borrow a book from the Amazon store on your paperwhite, the Kindle app, the Amazon app, and the Amazon store in a web browser. (Chapter 4 and Chapter 7)

- **Borrow a library book:** Borrow library books using Over-Drive's Libby app in participating US libraries (Chapter 7).

- **Transfer a book from your computer:** Download a book (free or purchased) from the web and then transfer it to your paperwhite (Chapter 7).

12.2 - Charging

Does ejecting your Paperwhite from your PC stop it charging?

No. Your paperwhite is charging if an orange light displays at its base. The *charging* icon will also be visible in the top right corner of the screen when you turn it on.

Can you plug the Paperwhite USB cable into an iPhone power adapter?

Yes you can. Any USB charger up to 9 watts will work (Chapter 3). Some low power USB outlets (eg. attached to old style keyboards) may not.

I've seen threads on forums saying that some big-brand higher wattage USB-C chargers work with the gen 11 paperwhite, but I have not personally tested any. I've also seen threads that warn against using no-name chargers. So, if you feel comfortable using a higher power USB-C charger, be sure to monitor your paperwhite closely the first few times you use it.

How do I charge my Paperwhite if my computer doesn't have

a USB port?

Use any charger with a USB connector. Most USB chargers will work.

How do I check the battery percentage on my Paperwhite?

Percentage-charged is shown in the top-right corner of the *Home* and *Library* screens, and in the *standard* toolbar when you're reading a book.

12.3 - Subscriptions

Is there a way to read my newspaper subscription on paperwhite?

Sort of. You can send news articles from your browser to your paperwhite (Chapter 7). Kindle newspapers and magazines were discontinued in mid-2023.

Do Amazon prime or Kindle Unlimited come bundled with my paperwhite?

No. These are separate subscriptions. If you sign up to Prime or Kindle Unlimited, make sure you sign up on the same account as your kindle so that your reading benefits flow through.

How many books can you download with kindle unlimited?

The Kindle Unlimited documentation says ten books, but lately I have been able to borrow twenty books at a time. After that, you'll need to return one to borrow another.

12.4 - The Amazon ecosystem

Can you delete your books once you're finished reading them?

Yes. Tap and hold the book thumbnail to launch the book menu. From the menu that pops up, *Remove download* keeps the book in the cloud but removes it from your paperwhite. *Permanently delete* removes it from the cloud and your device.

Do you have to be online to access the dictionary?

Initially yes. Once your paperwhite is setup and settled, no.

Will the kindle book I'm reading on my phone transfer to my paperwhite?

Yes. Anything you're reading in the Kindle app is synchronized to every other kindle device that's connected to your amazon account and connected to Wi-Fi.

When I've borrowed a kindle unlimited book using the kindle app on my iPhone, I've found that I need to open the book on my iPhone before it will download onto my paperwhite. Also, sometimes you may need to manually sync your paperwhite (label (17) in Figure 4-3).

Can I gift my kindle to someone with books already loaded?

Yes, but only if you leave it connected to your account. Kindle's *loan-to-anybody* functionality was discontinued in August 2022.

Can I lend a Kindle book to someone else?

Anyone with a kindle reader that's connected to your amazon account has access to your kindle library. Different members of my family use different kindle devices, and all are connected to the same account.

Occasionally there's a glitch and I need to go to the *Manage Content and Devices* area of my account (Chapter 9) to *Deliver* a book to a specific device.

12.5 - Hardware

Does my paperwhite power off automatically if I fall asleep while I'm reading?

Yes. After 10 minutes of inactivity your paperwhite goes to sleep. It uses very little battery in *sleep mode*. Some Kindle covers automatically put your Kindle to sleep when you close them and wake it up when you open them.

Why won't the charging cable I ordered from Amazon fit my paperwhite?

Most likely, you've ordered a charging cable for the wrong model of kindle. 10th generation paperwhites (and older) use MicroUSB. 11th generation kindles use USB-C type cables.

Should I upgrade my paperwhite?
⋮ > *Settings > Device Options > Advanced Options > Storage Management*

My decision to upgrade my old kindle to a paperwhite was an easy one. For me, the touchscreen, backlighting, and waterproofing features made the paperwhite a much more functional and flexible device than earlier models. However, the decision to upgrade from a gen 10 to a gen 11 paperwhite is a little more nuanced. Here's three things to consider. . .

- **The gen 10 and gen 11 paperwhite interface is almost identical:** Aside from a screen-warmth slider on the gen 11 paperwhite, the gen 10 and gen 11 interface is identical.

- **The hardware is different:** The gen 11 screen is slightly larger, the battery life is doubled, it uses a USB-C cable, it has improved lighting options, and a faster processor. You really do notice the performance difference, especially for VoiceView text to speech.

- **Memory model:** In the *Settings* menu, tap *Device Options*, then *Advanced Options* and then *Storage management* to see how much storage you use on your existing kindle. On my 32 GB model gen 10, the operating system uses around 5GB, but I only use around 1 GB for my books. I could easily upgrade to a smaller model gen 11. My usage pattern - I read mostly kindle unlimited books that I return after reading. I have ~150 books in my library. About equal parts fiction and nonfiction. I do not listen to audiobooks on my paperwhite.

I bought a gen 11 for my partner. It's fantastic to use, but I'm still happy to keep using my gen 10 for a bit longer.

12.6 - General questions

Does paperwhite use the open dyslexic font?
Aa > Font > Font Family > Open Dyslexic

Yes. You access it from the Aa icon in the Display Settings menu (label (26) in Figure 4-4)

Can I use wired headphones?

No. But you can use Bluetooth headphones (Chapter 8).

Can you play games on a paperwhite?

No. It's books only.

How to get the most from my paperwhite?

- **Use goodreads:** Create a profile in goodreads.com and start creating a list of books that you want to read.

- **Make yourself accountable:** Regularly update the status of the books you've read on the goodreads site.

- **Wish list:** Add books to your amazon wish list so you're notified if the price drops.

- **Set a Reading Challenge:** Make public the number of books you plan to read that year.

- **Monitor your reading habits:** Do this from the home screen of the kindle app on your smart device (this information is not displayed on your paperwhite or in the desktop app).

Does the paperwhite have a web browser?

Yes. You access it from the ⋮ icon in the home screen and library screen. It's often called an experimental browser, and there's good reason for that. The paperwhite's processor is not powerful enough to run a browser at the speed that desktops and smart devices can. However, your paperwhite's web browser is convenient for opening website links from a book you're reading.

Is my Paperwhite waterproof?

Your Paperwhite has an IPX8 waterproof rating. That means it can handle being fully submerged in one meter of fresh water for up to an hour (Gen 11 specs say 2 meters). So, you can use it in a swimming pool or bath without worrying about it getting damaged. The rating only applies to the device, and not the cable and other accessories.

The rating is intended to deal with accidental submersion. That doesn't mean that you should plan to take your paperwhite scuba diving with you!

The charging port is the weak link in the chain, so make sure it's completely dry before you try to charge it up.

How do I capture a screen?

To capture a screen, touch diagonally opposite corners of your paperwhite at the same time. You'll see the screen flicker and the screen capture will be saved to your paperwhite. If the screen doesn't flicker, your simultaneous taps haven't worked. Screen capture can be temperamental and frustrating. If you can't get it to work, here's some things to try. . .

- **Fingers too dry:** Try again. It may be that one of your fingers is too dry and the paperwhite didn't register it.

- **Technique:** You may be tapping and holding instead of doing a quick simultaneous tap.

- **Restart:** Restart your paperwhite (Chapter 3)

You transfer screen captures to your desktop computer using the USB cable that came with your paperwhite. You'll find your screen capture .png files at the root of your kindle's folder structure. From there you can cut and paste them to a folder on your desktop computer as you would with any other file. Be sure to "eject" your kindle from your desktop before disconnecting the cable.

What is Goodreads?

Goodreads is an amazon owned social network for book lovers. When its linked to your Amazon account (an option during your paperwhite setup), you can track your reading progress, rate and review books, and connect with other readers. You can only write reviews from the browser version or the goodreads app on your smart device.

To track your reading progress on goodreads, add books to your *currently reading* shelf in the *About This Book* item in the menu that launches from the ⫶ menu (label (3) in Figure 4-1) and update your progress as you read. This will allow you to see how far you have progressed in each book, and how much time you have spent reading.

Goodreads also has a social aspect. You can connect with other readers and share your thoughts and recommendations. You can follow other users, join groups with similar interests, and participate in discussions and challenges. All your activity gets shared with your connections.

Can I print a kindle book?

No. None of the Kindle apps allow printing, and copyright laws prohibit it. However, you can use the copy and paste functionality in your browser or Kindle app to copy and paste small sections of a book for research purposes.

Chapter 13

Finally

Thankyou so much for buying this book and allowing me to show you ways to get the most out of your paperwhite. Maybe, you now love your paperwhite as much as I love mine!

Don't forget the resources page at ianallanauthor.com/paperwh ite

If you feel up to doing something incredibly helpful to me, I would be so grateful if you would take the time to leave a review for the Kindle Paperwhite User Guide 2023 on its Amazon page or on its Goodreads page, or, if you're feeling incredibly generous, both. I'm an indie author, so I love and I appreciate every reader who takes the time to do that. Every review counts!

Made in the USA
Las Vegas, NV
16 September 2024

95370685R00075